Emerald City:
How Capital
Transformed New York

Emerald City:
How Capital
Transformed New York

Joseph Grosso

Winchester, UK
Washington, USA

JOHN HUNT PUBLISHING

First published by Zero Books, 2020
Zero Books is an imprint of John Hunt Publishing Ltd., No. 3 East St., Alresford,
Hampshire SO24 9EE, UK
office@jhpbooks.com
www.johnhuntpublishing.com
www.zero-books.net

For distributor details and how to order please visit the 'Ordering' section on our website.

Text copyright: Joseph Grosso 2019

ISBN: 978 1 78904 536 9
978 1 78904 537 6 (ebook)
Library of Congress Control Number: 2019954016

A CIP catalogue record for this book is available from the British Library.

Design: Stuart Davies

UK: Printed and bound by CPI Group (UK) Ltd, Croydon, CR0 4YY
US: Printed and bound by Thomson-Shore, 7300 West Joy Road, Dexter, MI 48130

We operate a distinctive and ethical publishing philosophy in
all areas of our business, from our global network of authors to
production and worldwide distribution.

Contents

For Louis Lister

Acknowledgments

Back in 1675 when Isaac Newton famously wrote in his letter to fellow scientist Robert Hooke, "If I have seen further, it is by standing upon the shoulders of giants," he perhaps didn't realize how much that sentiment also applies to writers. Anyone reading and writing about New York City has had the honor of standing upon the shoulders of many giants and luminous New Yorkers including Wayne Barrett, Robert Fitch, Juan Gonzalez, and Jack Newfield among many others. Their influence and inspiration on this work is obvious. This small book is an attempt to further their causes. And no book, great or small, could be completed without the support, not to mention tolerance, of family and friends, especially my wife Jingmin, and our two wonderful children, Heather and Christopher.

Chapter 1

From its inception New York has been a city of contradiction. In its early Dutch days as New Amsterdam it was a beacon of cultural tolerance when compared to surrounding New England, symbolized by the Flushing Remonstrance of 1657 (Flushing then known as "Vlissengen") that challenged director-general Peter Stuyvescent's suppression of Quaker settlers, yet its Dutch history featured two bloody conflicts and fairly consistent shady dealings with the indigenous population. In the mid-eighteenth century, New York was one of the first cities to grant voting rights to African-Americans who met property owning qualifications when just a few years before rumors of a widespread slave uprising (slaves made up about 20 percent of the city's population) sparked a witch hunt and series of executions, of both black and white persons, that compare with the more infamous episodes in Salem. New York was the first capital of the independent US despite the fact that it was the first city occupied by the British during the War of Independence (New Yorkers celebrated "Evacuation Day" for many years afterward). Nineteenth-century New York was a city of Irish and German immigrants while also being the city of the Know-Nothings. Far from being a liberal center of abolitionism, the civil war era featured a mostly slavery accommodating bourgeoisie up to the start of the war and later the very anti-black draft riots, then the largest urban insurrection in American history.

This continues to the current day. For decades now New York has been billed a city of renaissance and prosperity, its present constantly compared to "darker" days of the late 1970s and other periods. Yet New York's poverty rate (and near poverty rate) during the 1970s equaled the national rate (in the 1960s, New York's rate was two-thirds the national rate); it now dwarfs the national rate by more than 40 percent. As of 2016 New York's poverty was 19.5 percent. The poverty rate, along with the near poverty rate, officially up to $47,634 a year for a family of four, encompasses almost half the city. Large stretches of the city are more and more becoming a playground for millionaires and tourists, the waterfronts colonized by luxury condominiums. High-end buildings designed by star architects dot the landscape and celebrity chefs open restaurant after restaurant. New York is celebrated as one of the world's centers of diversity, and the city government celebrates New York's role as a sanctuary city, meanwhile the city has one of the most segregated school systems in the country. The Rust Belt has drawn the lion's share of media focus regarding the opioids epidemic, parts of New York have been hit as badly as anywhere – if the Bronx were a state (its half-million population makes it roughly equal to Wyoming) its rate of overdose deaths, 34 per 100,000 people, would be second only to West Virginia[1]. The Bronx has long been the poorest urban county in the United States. New York has some of the highest priced housing in the world, and a homeless population of over 60,000.

The process by which New York became safer and more glamorous while becoming poorer and less equal speaks to economic, political, and cultural dynamics that go back decades. For urban areas these dynamics can perhaps be broadly described as deindustrialization and gentrification. Obviously these dynamics are highly symbiotic and apply to cities far beyond New York; in fact they can probably be applied to some extent to every American city. As federal money has been withdrawn, cities are pitted against each other in a global economy. Cities that are said to have transitioned from an industrial-based economy (Pittsburgh, Seattle, San Francisco) are considered superstar cities whereas others are considered failures (Detroit, Baltimore, St. Louis). Urbanist Richard Florida describes the process as "winner-take-all" urbanism where cities fiercely compete for businesses. In 2018 this was seen in its most grotesque form with dozens of cities competing through very lucrative subsidy offers to win the honor of hosting Amazon's second headquarters, only to see Amazon in the end dividing its promised 50,000 jobs among two metro areas already considered "superstars," including New York where Amazon originally planned to build a headquarters in rapidly gentrifying Long Island City, Queens. The plan included $3 billion worth of subsidies for Amazon. One of New York's booming waterfronts, no other neighborhood in the country in recent years has added as many new apartments as Long Island City. According to a study by RENTCafe, since 2010 Long Island City has added nearly twice as many apartments as Downtown Los Angeles, the neighborhood that was second on the list[2]. The average income along the waterfront is $138,000. Fortunately, local opposition forced Amazon to back out of the deal.

Or cities compete in attracting what Florida calls the "creative class" through universities and infrastructure initiatives, and/or tourism. Prominent industries, such as technology and finance, despite their obvious global reach, tend to be highly concentrated in selected cities. The cities that win the game become playgrounds for tourists, urban professionals, and the global elite's lives of consumption, with immigrants and the working class providing the labor in the service economy. Those cities that fail sink further in economic stagnation, population decline, and poverty. According to the Brookings Institute, between 2010 and 2017 nearly half of the country's total employment growth occurred in 20 large metro areas, while the Economic Innovation Group reveals that from 2010 to 2014 five metro areas[3], New York, Miami, Los Angeles, Houston, and Dallas, produced as big an increase as the rest of the country combined (with the New York and Washington metro regions accounting for roughly half of the net increase across the country between 2007 and 2016)[4].

As the defeated Amazon deal illustrates, an important part of the process, at least from the point of view of private companies, is subsidies. According to a report by the Citizens Budget Commission, New York spent $9.9 billion on state and local development in 2018, up 17 percent from 2016. State costs were $4.8 billion, an increase of $965 million from 2016. Local tax expenditures increased $458 million[5].

For a majority of the twentieth century New York was a city of industrial workers. While the percentage of workers engaged in manufacturing peaked in 1910 at just over 40 percent, the overall number of workers engaged in manufacturing increased every decade in the first half of the century with the exception of Depression years of the 1930s. In the immediate aftermath of World War II, obviously the driver for pushing New York's manufacturing production to an all-time high, New York's workforce numbered 3.3 million of which fewer than 700,000 were professionals or managers. In 1950, though by then seven of the ten largest cities in the US had a higher percentage of their workforces engaged in manufacturing than New York, New York contained more manufacturing jobs than Boston, Detroit, Philadelphia, and Los Angeles put together[6].

Beyond the sheer numbers of New York's industrial economy was its uniqueness. Given New York's density and high land costs, its factories were much smaller than the vast Fordist factories of Pittsburgh and Gary. In 1947 manufacturing establishments employed on average 25 workers, less than half the national average of 59. When companies expanded and their production standardized, they would more often than not leave New York for roomier places. In New York manufacturing was diverse and flexible, a Silicon Valley of sorts that generated a disproportionate amount of US patents; at its peak there were more than 70,000 firms in various stages of production. Much of the production was specialized in areas such as machinery and custom-made jewelry. Its garment industry was well attuned to changing styles and trends. In absolute terms New York had a goods-producing economy of unprecedented size and complexity. Just as present day cities with thriving tech industries are known for their clusters of idea networks, flexibility, and spillover effects that combine to spur innovation so Joshua Freeman in *Working Class New York* describes New York's garment industry:

> In some cases versatility was a trait of individual businesses. In other cases it was a trait of constellations of firms, each of which in itself might be quite specialized. For example, the apparel industry was not really one industry but many...Within each of these sectors were jobbers, who designed and sold apparel and sometimes cut the needed material; contractors, who made apparel from material and specifications given them by others; and manufactures who performed both functions[7].

Of course, there is always a risk of romanticizing the past. Factory work can be back-breaking and post-industrial New York is a less polluted, healthier city. The very pro-corporate Mayor Bloomberg was on the forefront of good "nanny state" reforms such as banning smoking in restaurants and bars and trans-fats from city menus. However, there is no way around the increased poverty and inequality the economic transformation has unleashed. A basic source of economic inequality in cities stems from the division between professionals earning high (or at least very livable salaries) and the working class working in low-wage jobs in the service economy. Such is where manufacturing is missed. In 2013, manufacturing jobs in New York City paid $51,000 a year on average, compared with $25,416 for positions in retail, hotel, and restaurant sectors[8]. To get a nationwide sense of the American job picture consider that the largest private employers are currently low wage service sector jobs: Wal-Mart (fortunately outlawed in New York), Amazon, Kroger, Yum! Brands (the corporation that operates Taco Bell, KFC, and Pizza Hut), and Home Depot.

The national economic transformation had its origins in New York. And from the beginning city planning and policy was as large a factor as any other in making it happen. New York's famous 1916 zoning law, the first comprehensive zoning law in American history, was driven in part by the proximity of Manhattan businesses to the shopping district of 5th Ave. A century ago business in New York often meant factories and New York's center featured the Garment District. Factories paying lower rent threatened nearby property values. The zoning law established separate commercial, industrial, and residential districts in Manhattan (the outer boroughs were classified "unrestricted" meaning the three could be mixed). If separating residential and industrial districts has the defendable result of isolating industrial pollution to a limited extent, the zoning law also isolated industry and the working class.

The latter idea seems to have been on the minds of planners. Economist Robert Haig summarized it like this:

Some of the poorest people live in conveniently located slums on high-priced land. On patrician Fifth Avenue, Tiffany and Woolworth, cheek by jowl, offer jewels and jimcracks from substantially identical sites...A stone's throw from the stock exchange the air is filled with the aroma of roasting coffee; a few hundred feet from Times Square with the stench of slaughter houses. In the very heart of this "commercial" city, on Manhattan Island south of 59th street, the inspectors in 1922 found nearly 420,000 workers employed in factories. Such a situation outrages one's sense of order. Everything seems misplaced. One yearns to rearrange things to put things where they belong.

In 1929 the first Regional Plan Association (RPA) report was released. Founded in 1922, the RPA bills itself on its current webpage as "America's most distinguished urban research and advocacy organization" and "an indispensable source of ideas and plans for policy makers and opinion shapers across the Tri-state region." Its yearly conference is an event. The cornerstone of the RPA is seldom but vast plans it issues. There have been four in its history: The first in 1929, the second in 1968, the third in 1996, the most recent in November 2017.

Like practically all civic associations the RPA has been dominated by business and real estate interests. In 1929, under the leadership of planner Thomas Adams, there was the Rockefeller Foundation, powerful Brooklyn landowner FB. Pratt (son of the more famous Charles Pratt), major Queens landowner Charles G. Meyer, Robert De Forest, a former politician who owned much undeveloped land on Long Island, Dwight Marrow of Morgan Bank, also a director of New York Central Railroad, Frederic Delano, uncle of the future president and director of numerous railroads, and an officer from the Otis Elevator Company, elevators being a necessary technology for skyscrapers. The RPA project was funded largely by the Russell Sage Foundation – Russell Sage being the nineteenth-century finance and railroad baron, (and robber baron). After Sage died in 1906 his wife Margaret Olivia Sage established the foundation with a $10 million gift. The foundation was the main financer of the Forest Hills Garden, a wealthy, private neighborhood in Central Queens.

While intentionally trying to avoid using the word, the 1929 plan was an exercise in decentralization. The plan envisioned a sprawling collection of bridges and highways out of New York City. The George Washington Bridge (construction started in 1927, according to the RPA webpage, "Based on RPA's recommendation in the first regional plan, the Port Authority relocated a planned Hudson River crossing at 57th Street and replaced it with the George Washington Bridge at 178th Street"), the Whitestone Bridge (1939), the destructive Cross Bronx Expressway , the Henry Hudson Parkway, and the Verrazano

Bridge (1964 – RPA's webpage: "effectively completed the regional highway system that had been proposed by RPA in 1929"), were all built according to RPA proposals.

The same has been true for deindustrialization. The RPA's plan envisioned a Manhattan cleansed almost entirely of manufacturing below 59th Street, including the entire West Side below 14th Street. What was to remain were a few scattered pockets. Most crucially, the plan called for New York's port, the harbor being what gave New York its edge over early rivals Boston, Philadelphia, and Baltimore making it the largest city in the country (about three-quarters of the country's wholesale trade in the early 1950s was transacted through New York[9]), to be moved across the water to Elizabeth, New Jersey. This was all achieved.

Of course, none of it could be done overnight. Critics who underestimate the effect of the RPA plan due to the timeframe of its eventual achievement are misguided. Development is a long game, far beyond the whims of daily politics. The image needn't be one of mustache-twirling villains pulling strings in a sinister puppet show (though in the case of the Rockefellers it can be said that David and Nelson furthered John Jr.'s cause). The point is elite planning being realized in the long run and such planning is endemic and generational. In 1929 "globalization" wasn't a glamourous word and things like containerization weren't part of any vocabulary. Either the members of the RPA in 1929 were unbelievably prescient or simply interested in their own vision and interests.

To begin with the plan ran smack into the Great Depression then World War II. Tammany Hall, long the machine of the Democratic Party in New York, specialized in working-class patronage and served as a counterforce. The rise of the Reform wing of the Democrats in the early 1960s, signified by the reelection of Robert Wagner in 1961 after his break from Tammany, provided an opening. By then there had been other plans put forward in the same spirit of the 1929 plan. In 1958 the Downtown Lower Manhattan Association (D-LMA) was founded by David Rockefeller. Rockefeller would become president of Chase Bank 2 years later and move the bank's headquarters downtown to One Chase Manhattan Plaza. Robert Moses encouraged Rockefeller to develop a plan for the area leading to D-LMA's forming.

In 1961 the city put forward its second major zoning law (after the first in 1916). The 1961 Zoning Resolution substantially shrunk manufacturing zones in Manhattan. Heavy industry was to be moved to the outer boroughs and light manufacturing limited only to Manhattan's waterfronts. The central areas were cleared out as foreseen by the 1929 plan (the 1961 Resolution divides the entire city into commercial, residential, and industrial zones, not just Manhattan as in the 1916 Zoning). Despite still paying lip service to the importance of manufacturing to the city's economy, official policy was geared toward its elimination.

Like the RPA, D-LMA has from its inception been a vehicle for financial and real estate interests. Its webpage declares D-MLA to be "Downtown stakeholders committed to the vibrant business community." Other players in D-LMA's founding included G. Keith Funston, then head of the stock exchange, Henry S. Morgan of Morgan Stanley, and Fred Ecker of Metropolitan Life (Met Life was the mortgage holder for Rockefeller Center and a major real estate investor in New York). Its immediate purpose was to lobby for projects meant to expand the downtown financial district and build upper-class housing for its workers. Rockefeller had his eyes on what he termed "gray areas." "The main problem arises, not the populous core or on the outer fringes where growth is taking place, but in the gray areas between the two...these gray areas are left behind, not in the sense of being abandoned, but in the sense of enjoying the best or highest use[10]." This was an official way of saying smallish industrial lofts no longer had a place downtown.

Again this couldn't be an overnight affair and it is worth noting that the planners didn't get everything. The Lower Manhattan Expressway, a project originating with Robert Moses in the 1940s, and often described simply as a battle between Moses and Jane Jacobs (Jacobs chaired the Joint Committee to Stop the Lower Manhattan Expressway – the expressway would have run straight through Greenwich Village and SoHo cutting Washington Square Park into pieces) was defeated despite support from the D-LMA which argued the highway would provide efficient transportation to the planned high-rise buildings. Another project, a housing complex along the East River called "Manhattan Landing," never got off the ground, though the South Street Seaport, a shopping mall in the guise of an old port, was built in its place.

However the planners got plenty. A centerpiece was the World Trade Center (aka The Twin Towers). The World Trade Center was proposed in 1960 and opened in 1973, for a few years the towers were the tallest buildings in the world. For the infantile idea that the 9/11 attacks on the World Trade Center were somehow an attack on "capitalism," the World Trade Center site has always been owned by the Port Authority of New York and New Jersey. Founded in 1921, the authority is a joint state controlled and subsidized venture that operates the ports, the Holland and Lincoln Tunnels, and the George Washington Bridge, as well as running the city's two main airports (the authority pays the city rent for the airports). The most immediate results of the World Trade Center's development were the orchestrated transfer of New York's primary port to New Jersey, the accomplishment longed for by elite planners since the late 1920s, and the destruction of 30,000 manufacturing jobs along what was Radio Row, a 13-block stretch of small electronic businesses. It was state-directed deindustrialization. For much of their history, the towers were full of unprofitable state agencies and were a drain on the city's coffers. By 1979 the World Trade

Center cost the city $700 million in lost real estate taxes.

Over on the Westside stands Battery Park City. Built mostly on a landfill created from the debris of the World Trade Center's construction, Battery Park City, under the auspice of the Battery Park Authority, another public benefit corporation, is a 92-acre planned community along the Hudson River. The authority was established in 1969, the project has been built since the 1980s. The original idea was to nicely house Wall Street workers and this to some extent has been the case though families now make up an increasing portion of residents. Its dozens of acres of green space are highly touted, but prices remain well beyond most city residents.

The loss of the port undoubtedly accelerated New York's deindustrialization. It is a fact that by this time containerization was a reality reducing the size of the longshoreman's workforce. In 1954 over 35,000 men were registered with the Waterfront Commission. By 1970 there were 21,600[11]. New Jersey offered more open land for larger factories and more optimal rail connections for containers. However it is also true that the Port Authority, being courted by New Jersey, invested hundreds of millions in the New Jersey waterfront while New York, due to planning and political rivalry[12], in fairness the city was slow, for reasons of pride and cronyism, to allow the authority to take over its port, allowed its docks to become outdated. When money was eventually spent it was spent inefficiently (the Port Authority eventually did build a container port in Red Hook, Brooklyn. At 80 acres it can accommodate no more than 150,000 containers a year. Port Authority's four ports in New Jersey, encompassing over 2000 acres, move roughly 6 million annually). The result of all of this was that New York's deindustrialization came earlier and faster than the deindustrialization of other American cities. Between 1964 and 1976, the number of trucking and warehousing jobs increased nationally while dropping sharply in New York after 1970. Overall, more than 700,000 manufacturing jobs disappeared in New York between 1950 and 1990, an epoch when national factory employment actually rose by a third.

Conservative critics, as is always their wont, have pointed to high taxes as the driving force. Specifically a 1966 package of tax increases. The package was generally proposed by Mayor John Lindsay but necessarily approved by Governor Rockefeller and the state legislature – it is interesting to note that in the State Senate, then under Republican control, about an equal number of Republicans and Democrats voted for and against the bill (the State Assembly was more heavily Democrat and voted for it). The bill included a personal income tax starting at 0.4 percent topping at 2 percent, a flat tax commuter tax of 0.25 percent, a 25 percent jump in the stock transfer tax, and a general business tax that replaced the city's gross receipts tax[13].

There was plenty of justification for the increases. New York faced a budget deficit in the mid-1960s, and though certainly his reputation would be in tatters a decade later, Lindsay was credited at the time with saving the budget. With the new income tax it was necessary to balance it with a commuter tax. This was a period when the suburbs were all the rage and the city couldn't provide further incentives to the many that already favored suburbanization. The idea of the business tax change was to place more of the burden on profitable industries like finance and less on high-volume, low-margin industrial businesses such as printers and garment manufacturers. Under the gross revenue tax that was in place the burden was on such low-margin businesses and decades earlier LaGuardia had exempted banks, the city's most profitable industry. Therefore some reform was needed. Evidence suggests that in reality the initial tax of 5.5 percent was high enough to increase the burden on low-margin businesses. A 1974 study by the city's Budget Bureau estimated that between 1966 and 1971 the city lost 44,500 factory jobs it would not have if the tax burden had been less severe. It would be naïve to totally discount taxes. Yet assuming the Budget

Bureau's number is correct, taxes would hardly be the greatest factor. In the long run there is the context of the 1961 Zoning Resolution, the loss of the port, the planned expansion of the Central Business District. D-LMA's 1969 report celebrated that between 1957 and 1968 there were 26 buildings built 20 stories or higher. The building boom of the late 1960s-early 1970s saw over 66 million feet of office space added in Manhattan. Taxes were comparatively minor in their effect.

The term "gentrification" was coined by sociologist Ruth Glass in the introduction to her 1964 book *London: Aspects of Change*. Describing what she saw happening in Central London at the time, Glass wrote:

> One by one, many of the working class quarters of London have been invaded by the middle classes – upper and lower. Shabby, modest mews and cottages – two rooms up and down – have been taken over, when their leases have expired, and have become elegant, expensive residences. Larger Victorian houses, downgraded in an earlier or recent period have been upgraded once again…Once this process of "gentrification" starts in a district, it goes on rapidly until all or most of the original working class occupiers are displaced, and the whole social character of the district is changed[14].

Glass's coinage was ironically rooted in the class structure of the English countryside with its rural gentry, the well born, landed, "genteel" class that was just below the nobility. The term "gentrification" poked fun at the new urban gentry for its implicit anti-urbanism in their taste for the "natural" way of life that was apparent in so many of the Victorian home renovations – natural wood, open fires (such a critique remains obvious today)[15].

At the same time, or even a bit earlier, as Glass was

formulating the concept of gentrification in London, parts of Brooklyn were undergoing a similar dynamic. Today Brooklyn is a global brand, synonymous with gentrification, artists, hipsters, and techies – a transformation from a gritty past to the essence of urban chic. Central to this image is Brooklyn's large stock of brownstones that stand in the eastern and central sections of the borough. A single brownstone on the market fetches millions. However, most of these brownstones, a brownstone being a type of row house distinguished by the 4-to-6 inch thick sandstone veneer covering the building's front side, at the time they were constructed were cheap and mechanized. Suleiman Osman, in his book *The Invention of Brownstone Brooklyn*, writes that "while over time they would weather and develop richly unique surfaces, brownstones were in original design no more or less authentic than a Levittown Cape Cod."[16] At a time in the nineteenth century when the wealthy preferred marble or expensive stone, the sandstone of brownstones was a cheaper, mass-produced substitute. Built in a speculative frenzy many brownstones were shabbily built and quick to decay. How did cheap mass-produced structures become chic?

The neighborhood Brooklyn Heights was a starting point. In 1960 only 9 percent of 11,457 housing units in Brooklyn Heights were occupied by residents who arrived before World War II. A high percentage, 36 percent, arrived between 1958 and 1960[17]. In nearby Park Slope, a group calling itself the Park Slope Betterment Committee was founded in 1966 by Everett Ortner and began buying properties and advertising them through real estate brokers to white collar workers. The committee would soon have its own magazine The Brownstoner. Brooklyn Union Gas Company also got involved in renovating buildings at Prospect Place, a process known as "Cinderella Schemes," schemes that attempted to bring about change by stimulating private sector investment in threatened neighborhoods. Brooklyn Union's project was financed by the Federal Housing Association and

New York Savings Bank[18].

Park Slope's brownstones, while certainly not as grand as some of the upscale housing in Brooklyn Heights (New York's first suburb), were at first housing for Brooklyn's middle class. The expanding subway would pull the middle-class brownstoners further east in new neighborhoods such as Flatbush and Carnasie. The void was filled by working-class Irish and Italians with many of the brownstones subdivided. By the 1940s 75 percent of Park Slope's housing stock was rooming houses with absentee landlords. During the Depression, The Home Owners' Loan Corporation (HOLC) rated most of greater Brownstone Brooklyn, outside of Brooklyn Heights and the blocks surrounding Prospect Park (Brooklyn's version of Central Park), as Yellow ("Definitely Declining") or Red ("Hazardous "), i.e. redlined. It is significant to note that these classifications weren't only race-based but class-based – most of the area's inhabitants were white ethnics[19].

Of course, before there was any such brownstone movement the area that composed Brownstone Brooklyn was vast and diverse. It featured African-American neighborhoods such as Bedford-Stuyvesant and Fort Greene, the Gold Coast areas that encompassed the blocks of Brooklyn Heights surrounding Montague Street and parts of Park Slope, and whole sections where the descendants of European immigrants mixed with increasing Black and Puerto Rican populations. Since practically all of it was built long before the 1961 rezoning, industry mixed with residential areas.

According to Osman, the brownstoning pioneers, inspired perhaps by writers such as Truman Capote and Norman Mailer, who wrote about moving to Brooklyn from Manhattan, saw Brooklyn as an "urban wilderness." In a rebellion against the suburbs as well as the bland modernist mechanized buildings of Robert Moses' "slum clearance," Brooklyn's brownstones apparently offered an air of authenticity to go along with cheaper living space. Over in Park Slope there developed one of the largest communities of lesbians in the US. According to Tamar Rothenberg in an essay titled "And She Told Two Friends: Lesbians Creating Urban Space," this community came together through word of mouth networking.

It is important to point out that this early gentrification was an exception to general urban disinvestment. This was still the time of white flight and abandonment. Much of Brownstone Brooklyn was redlined. In 1972 the annual Brownstone Conference was established by a Brooklyn realtor, its initial purpose was to act as a brownstone bank as an alternative around redlining by mortgage companies and banks. Many brownstoners performed their own renovations (known as "sweat equity").

In gentrification literature such trends are broadly categorized as consumption-based explanations. Such explanations tend to be predominant in public discourse. Fast forward to present day New York and explanations for gentrification go something like this: When the crime rate in New York plummeted, the city became popular for more people, particularly young people, who perhaps grew up watching shows like *Seinfeld*, *Friends*, and *How I Met Your Mother*, as well as wealthier people. Increased demand makes housing costs higher – hence gentrification. As one neighborhood flips, the wave moves to the next, with subway lines (such as the L and G trains in Brooklyn) often cited as the wave's carriers. Accounts in the press are peppered with images of hipsters moving into former ghettos causing organic markets and foodie restaurants to open, and thereby rents to increase. It has reached the point where being a gentrifier itself has become a concept, even a responsibility – one to be handled delicately. A simple Google search brings up a host of posts along the lines of "10 Rules for being a Good Gentrifier," "20 Ways not to be a Gentrifier," "9 Tips to be a Good Neighbor if You're a Gentrifier," "Being a Neighbor in the Gentrification Era." Predictably this involves banalities such as talking to your neighbors," local shopping, volunteering, being courteous, etc.

Cultural trends will inevitably be a factor in any demographic trends. For one thing the average age of marriage has trended up for decades. As of 2017 the average age of a man getting married for the first time is 29.5, for women 27.4. In 1980 the average age for women was 22 (much of the marriage delay is due to college-educated professionals, the demographic that could be described as gentifiers. The working-class family is in shambles[20]). Never-married adults under 65 now make up 36 percent of the US population, up 10 percent from 1990. Cities are simply more interesting than suburbs for young single professionals, particularly if they have any money to spend. Of course, creative types have always called cities home. Back in 1989 sociologist Jon Caulfield argued that in a nation of suburbs: "Old city places offer difference and freedom, privacy and fantasy, possibilities for carnival...A big city is an encyclopedia of sexual possibility," a characterization to be grasped in its wider sense; the city is "the place of our meeting with the other."

Getting back to Brownstone Brooklyn, it is vital to recognize economics. As Osman writes:

> A dilapidated brownstone in Brooklyn Heights was astonishingly large and cheap in a suffocatingly tight market. To buy a new three-room cooperative apartment on the East Side of Manhattan in 1958 would require $15,000 and $175 in monthly maintenance fees. In Brooklyn Heights whole brownstones with four floors, several bathrooms, large kitchens, private stoops, and small yards were selling for as little as $30,000.[21]

An additional layer to consider is that in 1976 Park Slope had its highest rate of buildings, 7.1 percent, in 5+ quarters of tax arrears, meaning that the buildings most likely were abandoned.[22] Co-op and condo conversions began in 1977. Prior to 1977 there was no real interest from developers for such conversions. This is a credible reflection of what is known as the rent gap. In 1979 geographer Neil Smith published his theory of the rent gap. The basic point of the rent gap is quite simple: property ownership entitles for the collection of ground rent – the rent that owners are able to charge tenants to use (including live in) their property. This of course depends on a host of factors including location, size, municipal law, etc. The rent gap springs up when the ground rent that is actually being appropriated by the landlord, the capitalized ground rent, diverges enough from the potential ground rent, which is the maximum that could be gained if the land was being put to its "highest and best use," i.e. its most profitable use.

Put another way, the rent gap occurs when property values decline enough to be a good investment. Or perhaps even simpler, property becomes cheap enough to be enticing. Central to the process is disinvestment, decline, and stigmentation. Why else were Brooklyn's brownstone's a cheap, spacious investment? If the initial work was pioneering sweat equity, as Smith put it:

> Gentrification occurs when the gap is wide enough that developers can purchase shells cheaply, can pay the builders' costs and profit for rehabilitation, can pay interest on mortgage and construction loans, and can sell the end product for a sale price that leaves a satisfactory return to the developer.[23]

The recycling is the shift from disinvestment to reinvestment. It was disinvestment in its various forms that triggered the epoch known as the urban crisis. A generalized pattern of disinvestment according to the rent gap theory starts with the fact that new urban investment in a market economy is built to gain the highest return. Initially the price of property will reflect the value of the property's location, use, demographic, etc. As nearby development expands, the value of the investment may increase for a time. However, given that capital invested in land is anchored there, it is vulnerable to trends that upset the original local dynamic that built the neighborhood. Smith identified three broad factors of disruption: advances in the productiveness of labor (basically meaning advances in technology, landlords are left with buildings that were designed for best use decades ago), changing styles (including more efficient style techniques), and physical wear and tear. When the eventual and inevitable depreciation presents itself and neighborhoods become less economically competitive while buildings age and require maintenance landlords in certain neighborhoods most affected will develop less incentive to keep up investment in their properties (landlords differ from owner occupants in that they view their properties as strictly investments). In areas considered to be in decline, this is a rational, if gruesome, response.

Neighborhoods in decline attract poorer residents which can cause a spiral of further disinvestment as residents with means relocate. Landlords will create subdivisions within properties, essentially cramming tenants into spaces to extract as much rent as possible. The next step is for landlords to cease any upkeep of their properties and "milk" the property – make no investment, create smaller subdivisions, squeeze the most rent as possible from poor tenants. As the process is going on, banks and other financial institutions withdraw from such a neighborhood, classifying investments there as too risky, making mortgages and loans for businesses difficult to acquire. When landlords can no longer make a property profitable enough to cover taxes or upkeep the final step is abandonment. This increases popular stigmatization of the neighborhood as a ghetto. Abandonment is contagious as nearby landlords are motivated to do the same as adjacent properties are abandoned. The most extreme action a property owner could take is arson for profit – have the property burned down and collect insurance money.

Such decline in modern American history has, of course,

been bound to racial politics. As the Second Great Migration of African-Americans to northern cities commenced, a product of the mechanization of southern agriculture in the aftermath of the 1938 Agricultural Act and the expansion of the war economy during World War II, neighborhoods where black migrants settled were met with redlining.

In 1933, in the midst of the Great Depression, FDR signed the HOLC into law. HOLC's main purpose was to fund the refinancing of tens of thousands of mortgages in or at risk of foreclosure and it even granted low-interest rate loans to enable owners to recover lost homes. Between 1933 and 1935 HOLC supplied over $3 billion for over a million mortgages. HOLC made two signature contributions to the housing industry. First it introduced the long-term, self-amortizing mortgage with consistent payments for the whole term of the loan (previously mortgages were only for 5-10 years with the loan needing to be renewed leaving the owner at the mercy of the money market). Second, HOLC systemized appraisal methods across the country. The lasting dark side of this is that it introduced redlining. The basics of this were the HOLC dividing neighborhoods into four categories: green, blue, yellow, and red with red being neighborhoods unworthy of investment. It goes without saying that black neighborhoods, even neighborhoods with emerging black populations, were marked red, though as we've seen class in general was a major factor as well. These standards were adopted by the Federal Housing Authority when it came into being in June 1934. A manual for Federal Housing Authority (FHA) assessors gave instructions to reject loan applications for "all blocks in which there are more than 10 percent Negros or race other than white," adding also "areas where there are considerable number of Italians or Jews in the lower income group." As late as 1959, only 2 percent of all FHA insured housing loans were held by non-white borrowers.

There was also the phenomenon of blockbusting. In white

neighborhoods with declining property values, particularly if owners were occupying the properties, real estate agents would promote white flight by buying several homes and selling those to black buyers at exorbitant rates. This caused the surrounding houses to lose value quickly as white owners rushed to sell, hastening neighborhood decline. Popular notions about ghettoization and "culture" are so inherent that the racism and classism hardly generate an ounce of scrutiny. How often in popular conversation does one hear the word "ghetto" associated with banks, capital flight, or disinvestment?

Yet when the capitalized ground rent falls enough, particularly in a region with some level of population and employment growth, it can become potentially lucrative for investors and developers. As the capitalized ground rent falls, the potential ground rent is rising (again the difference between the two is the rent gap). Coinciding with cultural trends, which just as often aren't organic but created by economics and advertising, and subsequent herd behavior, such is the dynamic that brings gentrification.

Gentrification literature broadly divides gentrification into periods, or waves. First-Wave Gentrification began sometime in the 1950s, lasting until the economic recession of the early 1970s. Gentrification during this period was localized and sporadic. This was the time of white flight and suburbanization, making gentrification an exception to urban disinvestment (of course such disinvested neighborhoods were the target of early gentrification). Though that was the case this isolated gentrification had state support. There were the Housing Acts of 1949 and 1954 that provided federal funding to the clearing of blighted areas.

Second-Wave Gentrification began in the aftermath of the 1970s recession, during which time more neighborhoods underwent disinvestment making their declining property values attractive to developers and investors. Encompassing the post-recession 1970s through much of the 1980s (until Black Monday in October 1987 and the subsequent real estate crash), during this wave gentrification became anchored – along with resistance to it. In New York gentrification was solidified and expanded in downtown neighborhoods such as Tribeca, SoHo, and the Lower East Side. It was also the period when neoliberalism became entrenched as urban (and national) policy – what David Harvey describes as the shift from "urban managerialism" to "urban entrepreneurialism."[24] This shift was characterized by the rise of public-private partnerships and powerful subsidized developers. This period saw projects such as the South Street Seaport in New York and the expansions of the Inner Harbor in Baltimore and Faneuil Hall in Boston.

It was also the time New York became truly a global city in terms of finance and real estate (along with people as the 1965 Immigration Act took greater effect). By 1981 the US had become the leading recipient of foreign direct investment (FDI); previously the US had been the largest exporter of investment. The mid-1980s saw the US receive about 50 percent of global FDI, and about 60 percent of FDI by developed countries (in the 1970s only 9 percent of FDI by developed countries landed in the US).[25] For New York it was a time of sensational headlines about Japanese capital in light of many high-profile real estate deals including for the Tiffany Building (1986), the Exxon Building (1986), 666 Fifth Avenue (1987), and Rockefeller Center (1989).

After a pause during the early 1990s, Third-Wave Gentrification intensified the trends of the Second Wave. What distinguishes the Third-Wave is gentrification expanding out from the urban cores (in New York this meant gentrification expanding out from the downtown areas to other parts of Manhattan and the outer boroughs), corporate developers taking the lead in initiating gentrification (in previous periods pioneers would largely tame neighborhoods with state and police help before developers would stimulate large-scale gentrification), and increased state involvement (in New York, Times Square is a prime example – see Chapter 3). Neil Smith put this important distinction succinctly: "Most crucially, real estate development becomes a centerpiece of the city's productive economy, an end in itself, justified by appeals to jobs, taxes, and tourism."[26] The Third-Wave also saw anti-gentrification movements more marginalized.

A Fourth-Wave has been posited by some scholars to encompass the housing bubble of the early 2000s. The loosening of mortgage lending with the symbiotic Wall Street securitization flooded cities with capital. In New York mortgage commitments for condos and single-family homes grew from $14 billion in 2000 to $46.9 billion in 2003.[27] The housing bubble's inevitable bursting and ensuing foreclosure crisis left more properties open to be bought up by private equity and developers. If Second-Wave gentrification saw the emergence of the global city, the aftermath of the financial crisis saw it grow exponentially. Foreign and national corporate buying in the top 100 recipient US cities exceeded $600 billion in major acquisitions from mid-2013 to mid-2014 and $1 trillion in 2015. In New York foreign corporate buying of properties increased by 68.5 percent from 2013 to 2014.[28] We've also seen clear examples of "disaster capitalism," the wholesale remaking of spaces in the aftermath of a natural disaster (of course the term "natural disaster" is a misnomer, such events cause the most damage in places already gutted by politics and poverty), most prominently of course in post-Katrina New Orleans which was immediately a target for an immediate full-scale conservative reconstruction[29].

New York's modern epoch covers all the waves of gentrification. This can be seen by highlighting some prominent examples.

SoHo

The period from the late-1940s to the mid-1960s was the era of Robert Moses and urban renewal. Plus as we saw, David

Rockefeller's D-LMA saw downtown as a prime target for redevelopment given its proximity to Wall Street and the predominance of "gray areas" of light manufacturing. The Lower Manhattan Expressway proposal was a constant presence for years. Smack in the middle of all of this was SoHo (named for the neighborhood being south of Houston Street). In 1962 SoHo was featured in a planning study by the progressive City Club titled *The Wastelands of New York*. The study argued that the area was a commercial slum in need of better use. The redevelopment proposals at the time were middle-income housing. Two housing proposals were put forward that same year, one by Manhattan Borough president Edward R. Dudley, the other by a civic group called MICOVE. MICOVE billed itself as "an association of 5000 families in search of homes." Its plan for SoHo was a 31-acre development project.[30]

Fortunately SoHo's industry had defenders. In response to the MICOVE proposal, which had predictable construction union support, the New York City Planning Commission (CPC) commissioned a study by University of Pennsylvania professor Chester Rapkin. Rapkin's study, published in 1963, argued that the neighborhood's industry was an important and viable part of the city's economy, as well as, crucially when deindustrialization was increasing, a job provider for minorities. Rapkin found that wages in SoHo's industries compared favorably to similar industry nationally. The CPC would issue its own report shortly thereafter seconding Rapkin's conclusion by coming out strongly against urban renewal in SoHo, proclaiming in its report that the city "in its own economic self-interest and out of clear moral obligation must scrutinize very carefully any proposal involving further displacement of industry."

SoHo industrialized in the second half of the nineteenth century. Prior to the expansion of industry, SoHo served as Manhattan's first red light district as well as a spot for high-end shopping. As development spread further uptown, manufacturing, being at the time more profitable, displaced the stores, theaters, and hotels. These enterprises moved further uptown where they remain in and around Times Square and 5th Avenue. Given the age of much of SoHo's industrial buildings decades later, industry certainly faced challenges (recall the earlier point about buildings' designs having best uses for decades before). These challenges were primarily an issue of space. Buildings in New York are high, i.e. vertical, rather than wide. For loft factories this means elevators are critical and with multi-floor factories or buildings with numerous businesses this could mean long waits. Given the density of Manhattan streets, in a time when industries were moving to the sprawling suburbs, trucks had no off-street loading spaces and only a limited amount of trucks loaded at a time.

Yet according to Rapkin's study many of the businesses in SoHo were profitable. As of 1962 only 10 percent were in business for less than 5 years. More than 75 percent of businesses were more than 10 years old, a third of these were in business over 20 years. However, while on one level industry in SoHo had support against the urban renewal machine, on another level the city, despite recognizing the importance, never produced a plan to help industry survive in the long term[31]. Instead the neighborhood experienced disinvestment. Rapkin's data showed that disinvestment increased greatly after World War II (in keeping with the rent gap theory). Institutions, in this case banks, insurance companies, savings and loans companies, that generated 75 percent of all funding in first mortgages on SoHo's industrial lofts before 1945, decreased their commitment to 51 percent in 1945-49, 36 percent in 1950-54, 17 percent in 1955-59, and 11 percent in 1960-62.[32] In her classic work *Loft Living*, Sharon Zukin provides a sample taken of 34 buildings, the mortgage histories of which showed practically zero new financing between 1945 and 1959 before financing picked back up in the mid-1960s. Disinvestment also greatly affected the rail freight service that local industry depended on preventing the service's modernization.[33] Given the staying power of the businesses that Rapkin's study observed, it is difficult to believe serious planning and investment by the city and state wouldn't have made some difference toward fulfilling the Committee for Public Safety's (CPS) recommendation that deindustrialization be stemmed.

Zukin later notes:

> Moreover, by the middle of the 1970s, manufacturing tenants started to complain vociferously – to CPC, to the mayor, to anyone who would hear them – that their landlords deliberately created and maintained vacancies in order to facilitate residential conversion.[34]

In December 2016 a study was published in the journal *Urban Studies* that cast doubt on the artists-led gentrification narrative, finding that "the standard arts-led gentrification narrative is too generalized or simply no longer applicable to contemporary arts-gentrification processes."[35] However, it was in SoHo where this narrative first emerged as the arts were certainly the face of SoHo's transformation. As the industrial economy was undergoing disinvestment, the art economy was transforming. By the mid-twentieth century New York had established itself as the world capital of art. Interest in modern artists was growing, and art dealers (dealers open galleries) assumed a greater role in the industry that was expanding as collecting became more popular. Whereas in previous times the art industry was centered in Midtown near its wealthy patrons, such trends contributed to artists and especially galleries looking for cheap, open space. SoHo's lofts emerged as an arts center. The scale of the transformation can be measured by the sheer number of galleries that opened. The years 1964, 1966, and 1967 each saw one gallery open. The year 1968 had four openings (including the soon famous Paula Cooper Gallery), 1969 had six (including Ivan Carp's OK Harris Gallery), 1971 had nine, in 1972 there were 11, the same in 1974, 1973 had 13, and 1975 saw 18 gallery openings[36]. It was perhaps the birthplace of "industrial chic," an aesthetic that claims the "hip" look and feel of industry minus actual industry.

Just like the brownstones in Brooklyn were mass-produced structures meant to imitate wealth that eventually were craved by wealthy buyers, so too the cast iron facades of SoHo. Cast iron structures were easy and inexpensive allowing owners to imitate wealthy designs. Ironically much of both facades are now protected under historic preservation districts. Certainly not what their builders would have envisioned. The first of numerous protected areas in Brooklyn was designated in Brooklyn Heights in 1965. SoHo's designation came about in 1973 and was expanded in 2010.

SoHo's artists would become their own organizing force, first for the right to live in lofts, officially this was illegal in the early years but largely unenforced, the Loft Law requiring landlords to bring living spaces up to a certain residential code wouldn't be passed until June 1982 (the Loft Law also provided a measure of compensation for manufacturing firms who were displaced by residential conversions to assist in possible relocation), then later on against further gentrification that the art industry had played a role in establishing. In another irony the 1982 Loft Law led to the displacement of many artists, some of whom didn't have leases for their lofts. By that point, with SoHo's cool aura as a recognized brand, landlords were able to significantly raise rents. SoHo now boasts some of the most valuable real estate in New York. As of June 2018, Zillow lists the median home price there as $3,925,000.

Williamsburg

A video published on December 31, 2017 by CurbedNY couldn't

have been more telling if its creators actually tried. The video was a promo for a new large apartment building called 325 Kent. With 522 units, the $3 billion project is the first of three planned buildings. What makes the project prominent is that it is being built on the remains of the old Domino Sugar Refinery; built in 1882 it was once the largest sugar refinery in the world. The plant closed in 2004, only 3 years after its 300 workers (at the beginning of the twentieth century the plant employed 3000 workers) engaged in a 20-month long strike. Represented by the International Longshoremen Association, the workers struck to preserve sick days, protect seniority, prevent subcontracting, and stop layoffs.

The Village Voice at the time described the strikers like this:

They were a polygot crew, proud of their diversity: whites with Italian, Russian and Irish last names; Hispanics and native-born and Caribbean blacks. Many were women. They called themselves the United Nations. Their average age was late forties. Most had spent their entire working lives inside the hulking red brick plant with the huge smokestack dominating the Brooklyn shore by the Williamsburg Bridge.[37]

For 9 months not a single worker crossed the picket line – though one, a 62-year-old Russian survivor of a Nazi work camp, slit his wrists after another day on the line. In the end, however, the workers settled for a contract that contained the provisions that led to the strike, a loss greatly helped along by the fact that the plant's owners were able to almost reach full capacity with replacement workers (in contrast to a strike in 1992). Soon after the strike the plant's owner at the time, the British conglomerate Tate & Lyle, sold two plots of land on the property to developers and then sold the plant itself to Florida Crystals. Despite proclaiming a commitment to keeping the refinery open, shortly after a city rezoning proposal was made public, it was announced the plant would close.

The refinery building itself will soon be an office complex. Meanwhile the surrounding apartments, as per the CurbedNY promo, are "outfitted with hardwood floors, in unit laundry, and gorgeous views. There is a landscaped courtyard, lounge, gym, and a 7000 square foot shared roof deck." The main triumph according to the ad is: "This project highlights Williamsburg's transformation from an overlooked industrial zone to one of the country's most expensive neighborhoods."

In the summer of 2018, Domino Park, a 5-acre park along the waterfront, opened to the public. Besides featuring an elevated catwalk designed by the same company that designed the much ballyhooed Highline in Manhattan, the park contains what is being called "Artifact Walk" – a five-block stretch displaying over 30 pieces of machinery salvaged from the refinery.

If a feature of Third-Wave gentrification is the expansion of gentrification beyond the central core of a city, no neighborhood provides as prominent an example as Williamsburg, Brooklyn. Named by Richard M. Woodhall (the area's first developer) in 1800 after the soldier and surveyor Colonel Jonathan Williams (grandnephew of Benjamin Franklin), Williamsburg was originally used as a kind of waterfront suburb for the wealthy attracting the likes of Commodore Vanderbilt and William Whitney. Woodhall would go bankrupt early and the economic crisis of the mid-1830s slowed down real estate speculation; however as industrialization spread, the area was incorporated into Brooklyn in 1855, the same waterfront, along with the nearby Newton Creek, that drew the elite also brought industry.

Pfizer launched in Williamsburg in 1849. The Havemeyer and Elder sugar refinery (later Domino) opened their plant in 1856. Numerous brewers (Rheingold, Schafer) opened in the same period. The opening of the Williamsburg Bridge in 1903 brought a flood of working-class people fleeing the crowded Lower East Side and established a permanent symbiotic relationship between the two neighborhoods. The open space in Williamsburg didn't last long. By 1917 Williamsburg had some of the most densely populated streets in New York. Perhaps no other neighborhood in the city had more industrial workers. A large Jewish population, particularly Hassidic, along with Italian and Polish populations filled the area starting in the early 1900s. By the 1950s Puerto Ricans and Dominicans began to create what would become one of the largest *barrios* in the city. In their 1939 Guide to New York City, the Federal Writers' Project (a project meant to give writers work during the Depression under the Public Works Administration) labeled Williamsburg (along with next-door Greenpoint) as "virtually unrelieved slums."

The era of urban renewal brought large-scale change. Like many Brooklyn neighborhoods the construction of the Brooklyn-Queens Expressway cut through Williamsburg, uprooting many two- and three-family homes and leaving an empty gash. The expressway would become a perceived local barrier dividing Williamsburg and Greenpoint. Several public housing projects were built. The Williamsburg Houses (1938) were the first large-scale housing projects in Brooklyn; several others were built in ensuing years including Cooper Park Houses (1953) and Hylan Houses (1960).

In 1961 Williamsburg had an estimated 93,000 manufacturing jobs. Even by the turn of the twenty-first century, Community Board 1, where Williamsburg is located, had 55.9 percent of its land area zoned for industrial uses – this compared with only 13.2 percent for New York as a whole. The deindustrialization that swept the city certainly lowered the number of jobs and illegal residential conversions began to bubble up somewhat in the 1970s.

A 1987 study by the Department of City Planning found residential conversion in every manufacturing district but also found that Williamsburg was one of only eight manufacturing districts to gain manufacturing jobs at the time the study was conducted. The report concluded (echoing the report 2 decades earlier in SoHo) that: "Despite citywide job losses in the industrial sector, employment in the study area is increasing, demonstrating the underlying stability and strength of this key industrial area."[38]

Gentrification began to take off in the 1990s. As gentrification infected the Lower East Side, inevitably it spread to Williamsburg. The now mythical "L Train" brought artists and hipsters priced out of Manhattan. Prices in parts of Williamsburg began to soar by the late 1990s, particularly along Bedford Avenue and the surrounding environs. It became clear the waterfront would soon be a focus. For years community groups in Williamsburg and Greenpoint organized to revitalize the waterfront, eventually submitting plans under Section 197-a of the city charter that allows communities to submit plans for official approval. The plans called for a mix of low-to-mid-rise housing, long the basis for neighborhood housing, which would remain affordable to the local working-class population, along with the preservation of industry. The plans were approved, with some changes, by the city council around 2001. Tom Angotti, professor of Urban Planning at Hunter College, described what came next:

> Ever since the City Council voted for the Greenpoint and Williamsburg, in 2001, they have failed to lift a finger to implement them. City agencies went into hiding. There were no budget requests to create public access on the waterfront, no initiatives to preserve industry, and no new housing. Instead the city turned the other way as developers illegally converted industrial properties to unaffordable lofts, and did little to stop the legal conversions.[39]

Instead what came a few years later was a massive rezoning that would create vast developer wealth with the stroke of a pen and reform the waterfront into a luxury product. The community was able to get some concessions on affordable housing under the banner of inclusive zoning – often not binding during the Bloomberg years and just as often beyond working-class wages, and only available by winning an application lottery (over 80,000 people applied for the "affordable" housing at 325 Kent). Much of the rezoning fell under "mixed use," meaning landlords had the discretion for either industry or residential, giving landlords an incentive to build upper-class housing (the timing of the rezoning also incentivized developers to quickly build taller buildings in blocks that would be downzoned by the rezoning). The remaining number of industrial jobs in Williamsburg, which was still high compared to New York as a whole, halved from 2000 to 2009. According to a report conducted by city controller Scott Stringer, the Hispanic population in Williamsburg incredibly fell by 16 percent from 2000 to 2015.[40]

While gentrification was ongoing at the time of the rezoning given Williamsburg's proximity to Lower Manhattan, rezoning acted as an accelerant for rents everywhere in Williamsburg. As the waterfront filled with luxury development and prices continually rose, gentrification spread to Bushwick.

The Fires

Located east of Williamsburg and bordering Queens to the north and Bedford-Stuyvesant to the south, Bushwick's trajectory is even starker than Williamsburg's. Up to the early 1960s Bushwick was a neighborhood of German and Italian-Americans, communities that dated back to the nineteenth century. A combination of white flight to the suburbs, Puerto Rican and Dominican migration, and urban renewal projects in other parts of Brooklyn, notably in East New York and Brownsville, creating a displaced population that settled in Bushwick, quickly flipped the neighborhood demographics. During the 1960s Bushwick went from being 90 percent white to 60 percent Latino and Black, with a smaller Italian population remaining in the northern part of the neighborhood. By the late 1970s well over half of Bushwick's population was Hispanic.

Of course, the problem was such demographic trends coincided with other trends. Bushwick's industrial economy was sinking. At the height of the era of breweries in Brooklyn, Bushwick had more than any neighborhood. By this time all were closing or reducing staff. The Evergreen Brewery closed in 1955, Rheingold, the last large holdout, closed in 1976. A large number of the knitting mills along Wyckoff Avenue were closing. As poverty increased the local commercial economy declined.

Housing also saw deterioration. In the early 1970s the neighborhood was hit by a scandal involving FHA funds. The idea of FHA loans is to federally insure loans to low-income buyers. In this case realtors teamed up with bankers to secure inflated amounts of insurance with false paperwork (even for some buyers who were completely made up). A realtor would get a property for cheap, exponentially raise the selling price to sell it to a poor, minority buyer (who would obviously have less choice when it came to where to live), and file the false paperwork (paying off an FHA credit inspector if necessary). When the mortgage payments couldn't be paid the FHA paid off the balance. The huge amount of defaults left realtors collecting millions in insurance from the government while thousands of people lost their homes – in Brooklyn as a whole this racket added up to $200 million in fraud. About 500 of Bushwick's 12,000 buildings ended up abandoned as a result.[41]

Another blow came from bungled urban renewal. Up to that point Bushwick, unlike nearby Williamsburg and Bedford-Stuyvesant, hadn't been targeted for urban renewal projects. The city planned to tear down two square blocks of two-family houses to construct four 14-story housing projects along with a school and community center. Predictably, whatever its potential merits, the project met community resistance. By this time urban renewal justly had bad connotations with the public. Realtors stoked fear of the imminent arrival of more poor minorities. Community opposition was overruled and the land was cleared. However, the funding collapsed and the project was shelved leaving the neighborhood with the worst of all worlds: clearance without new housing. For over a decade a large trash-filled lot stood empty.

Abandonment, and the accompanying squatting and structural decline, brings down property values. The decline cycle expanded as many now absentee landlords in Bushwick began to invest less money in upkeep. With much of Bushwick's central core housing being wood-framed, featuring cock-lofts, roof spaces open from one building to another (originally built for ventilation), it wasn't long before there was an epidemic of fires. More demolished, burned, and abandoned structures lead to more. On some blocks every building was abandoned or demolished. Crime rose and by the mid-1970s Bushwick was a ghetto. In 1976 the two ladder companies working the neighborhood, Ladder 124 and Ladder 112, ranked first and second in the city for fire runs.[42] Considering the mid-1970s was a time of economic crisis for New York, the severe cutbacks in city and local services made many neighborhoods tinderboxes. During such times a spark inevitably turns up.

On July 13, 1977 at 8:37pm a bolt of lightning hit the Buchanan South substation located along the Hudson River. Substations hold the very big transformers that convert high-voltage electricity that generators produce into low-voltage electricity used in homes and businesses. Despite being designed to ground such lightning strikes, the one that night got through tripping two circuit breakers. The breakers did open the high-voltage lines as they were supposed to do to isolate the problem until the fault dissipated. This happened in under a second; however, because of a loose locking nut and a circuit that had been removed for upgrading not being replaced, the breaker didn't close to allow power to resume flowing.

Eighteen minutes later another lightning strike at the Sprain Book substation in Yonkers knocked out two transmission lines. Just over a half hour later, after futile attempts by Con Ed workers to stabilize the system, at 9:27 the largest generator in New York, Ravenswood 3, shut down and the lights in New York went off. Unlike the earlier 1965 blackout, which involved other states and affected New York unevenly, or the 2003 blackout that stretched from parts of Connecticut to Ontario, Canada, the 1977 was a New York affair. And unlike the other blackout it wasn't to be a peaceful affair. The power went off at a time that ensured total darkness yet was early enough for people to still be awake. For a city on its back from years of disinvestment and budget cuts, with unemployment in poor neighborhoods high, the timing couldn't have been worse.

The looting started immediately. At least 31 neighborhoods suffered significant damages, assisted in part by a police order that all city cops immediately report for duty yet ordering officers to report to the nearest precinct rather than their regular precinct. With most officers living in Long Island, Queens, or Staten Island many officers sat idle in the early hours of the blackout before being redeployed. Plus given the low morale of the force and its tense relationship with the city over funding cuts, many officers simply didn't show up. As the looting peaked after midnight, 40 percent of the force, around 10,000 officers, hadn't checked in[43].

When the dust settled thousands of stores were damaged, 1000 fires were reported, and more than 3,700 people were arrested. The Upper West Side up through Harlem and the Bronx were hard hit (for an anecdote the Bronx's Grandmaster Caz credited the looting of electronic stores with helping the spread of hip-hop, claiming "There was a large amount of DJs after that because equipment became more accessible.") No part of the city was hit harder than Brooklyn, no neighborhood suffered more damage than Bushwick. If Harlem and the South Bronx were already symbols of urban despair, the blackout put Bushwick on that map. Over 100 stores along Broadway, the area's main shopping street, were gutted, the looting lasting until the next day. Making matters worse, 5 days after the blackout an abandoned knitting mill on the corner of Knickerbocker Avenue caught fire. Known as the All Hands Fire, the blaze destroyed 30 buildings leaving 250 families homeless. All in all, as a result of abandonment Bushwick's population declined by a calamitous 32.9 percent from 137,900 in 1970 to 92,487 in 1980.[44]

As for the Bronx, it was only a couple of months after the blackout that President Carter made his surprise trip there. Carter, in New York for United Nations meetings, made the unannounced trip to display a commitment to cities. As the presidential motorcade made its way to its final stop on Charlotte Street it rode past chants of "Give us money" and "We want jobs." Carter stepped out of his limousine twice to speak to locals to proclaim the need for Federal help but offered no specific commitment. After returning to the United Nations Plaza Hotel Carter was quoted as saying:

> It was a very sobering trip for me to see the devastation that has taken place in the South Bronx in the last five years. But I'm encouraged in some ways by the strong effort of tenant groups to rebuild. I'm impressed by the spirit of hope and determination by the people to save what they have. I think they still have to know we care.[45]

A few weeks later viewers of Game 2 of the 1977 World Series were given a live view of the devastation that by then had plagued the Bronx for years. An hour before the Yankees and Dodgers took the field an abandoned schoolhouse a few blocks from Yankee Stadium caught fire. As fall winds fanned the flames dispatchers were initially able to send only one engine to combat the blaze and despite a second alarm nearby companies were too busy fighting other fires to respond. Howard Cosell never did utter the famous phrase attributed to him of: "Ladies and Gentlemen the Bronx is burning"; however, Cosell did note that President Carter had only recently visited the same area.

The decline that brought the Bronx to international notoriety follows the familiar script. Starting with the opening of New York's first subway line in 1904 the Bronx was a refuge for working- and middle-class families from the city's crowded downtown neighborhoods. The Grand Concourse, open to traffic in 1909, modeled on the Champs-Elysees in Paris, stretched originally from 161st Street to Bronx Borough Hall. In 1923 Yankee Stadium opened a few blocks away, just a short trip from the swanky Concourse Plaza, not far from Loew's Paradise Theater. Opened in 1929 the $4 million Paradise Theater was the city's grandest theater in an era of movie palaces.

Starting in the late 1940s, Puerto Ricans working in industrial jobs in Port Morris and Mott Haven began to join the first- and second-generation Italian, Irish, and Jewish families. Redlining took hold in some Bronx neighborhoods much like it hit other solid working-class neighborhoods. As the housing stock began to age and worsen as a result, around this time the "South Bronx" came into being, the area became a prime target for the urban renewal machine.

It was in the Bronx where Robert Moses' free hand caused its greatest disruption. Starting in 1950, the Bronx, along with Harlem, received a vast effort of slum clearance along with one of the highest concentrations of public housing in the city. Even more predominantly in the Bronx was the construction of highways. The Cross Bronx Expressway, built between 1948 and 1963, mainly to bring traffic through the Bronx to Westchester rather than into the Bronx, was perhaps the most destructive urban-renewal project in New York's history, it carved a wedge through the heart of a dozen neighborhoods, displacing at least 60,000 people. East Tremont never fully recovered. The 6-mile long Bruckner Expressway tore through Bruckner Boulevard, once the major commercial strip of the East Bronx. Between the Cross Bronx and the Bruckner is the little used 1-mile long Sheridan Expressway. That project also displaced thousands. The Major Deegan, the Bronx River, Sawmill, and Hutchinson River parkways as well as the Throngs Neck Expressway and New England Thruway crisscross the borough.

After a period in the 1960s when the increasing plight of cities briefly became a national issue, symbolized by the Johnson administration's War on Poverty, cities landed in a period of crisis. In New York, with Federal aid increasingly withdrawn under the Nixon administration, deindustrialization in full swing, helped in no small part by city planning, a national economic recession, and white flight all but completed, the urban crisis reached a peak. Writing in the *New York Times* in 1976, New York's Housing and Development Commissioner Roger Starr outlined a vision of what he called "planned shrinkage." He wrote, "Essentially, planned shrinkage is a recognition that the golden door to full participation in American life and the American economy is no longer to be found in New York." Declaring that "Large parts of the Bronx south of the Cross Bronx Expressway are virtually dead," Starr lamented that: "Yet the city must still supply services to the few survivors, send in the fire trucks when there are fires, keep the subway station open, even continue a school." Arguing that New York with two million less people would be an improvement, Starr called for "internal resettlement" arguing that: "The role of the city planner is not to originate the trend of abandonment but to observe and use it so the public investment will be hoarded for those areas where it will sustain life...The stretches of empty blocks may then be knocked down, services can be stopped, subway stations closed, and the land left to lie fallow until a change in economic and demographic assumptions makes the land useful once again."[46]

In a speech around the same time, Starr brought further

insight into his vision: "We should not encourage people to stay where their job possibilities are daily becoming more remote. Stop the Puerto Ricans and the rural blacks from living in the city...reverse the role of the city...it can no longer be a place of opportunity...Our urban system is based on the theory of taking the peasant and turning him into an industrial worker. Now there are no industrial jobs. Why not keep him a peasant?"

It is questionable if "planned shrinkage" ever was official policy in New York. Starr was forced to resign after the *Times* article (conveniently he went on to write for the *Times* full time). Though however extreme his vision was, it was by no means an outlier. Decentralization, not quite the same as dispersal but with some overlap, was favored Cold War planning – dense urban populations are easier to bomb than sprawling suburban populations. Investment banker and chairman of the Municipal Assistance Corporation (MAC), the corporation formed to sell city bonds in the midst of the financial crisis, Felix Rohatyn had a plan to blacktop much of the South Bronx. "Take a 30-block area, clear it, blacktop it, and develop an industrial park with the whole linkage of tax, employment financing incentives already in place."[47] Several years earlier, Daniel Patrick Moynihan, then serving as Nixon's Advisor for Urban Affairs and soon to be New York's senator, infamously urged a policy of "benign neglect" in a January 1970 memo. Moynihan would later attempt to clarify what he meant by that yet in the context of the Nixon administration's cutting of urban funding and Southern Strategy it may be safe to assume how it was received internally.

Whatever the extent planned shrinkage seeped into the minds of New York's planners, the city government's actions could be described as de facto planned shrinkage. On January 8, 1968, Mayor John Lindsay held a press conference to announce the creation of the New York City-RAND Institute. The purpose of the partnership with RAND was to study the city's housing, police, health, and fire departments. Lindsay had been elected in 1965 on a platform of reform, one pillar of which was the reorganization of the city's bureaucracy. Despite some initial success, the Lindsay administration was able to balance the budget and Lindsay himself received credit for his handling of riots in Harlem in 1967 and 1968 (the latter in the aftermath of Martin Luther King Jr's murder), yet it was clear the city's problems weren't going away. It wouldn't be long before the city's budget woes would return with a vengeance. Lindsay already faced a transit workers strike on his first day in office and a Teachers' Union strike in September 1967. It turned out at the time of the press conference announcing the RAND partnership that Lindsay was a month away from the 9-day Garbage Strike.

Fortunately, RAND got basically nowhere with the police and housing departments (one short-lived initiative was to split up partners on patrol). However, the one department that was receptive was the fire department. The department's Fire Chief at the time was John O'Hagan. O'Hagan would also be named Fire Commissioner by Lindsay in 1973 (Fire Chief is the operational lead, the Fire Commissioner oversees the whole department – O'Hagan was only the second man to hold both positions at once). To this point, O'Hagan's career could be fairly described as illustrious. Under his leadership the FDNY instituted reforms and technology such as fire-retardant work uniforms, annual medical tests for fire fighters, first aid masks, and "cherry picker" tower ladders that could reach above seven floors. O'Hagan was the main force behind the 1973 Local Law 5; at the time it passed the most comprehensive high-rise fire safety law in the country. Under O'Hagan's watch the FDNY also saw its first female applicants. Such progressive thinking led O'Hagan to see the appeal of advanced statistical analysis of the kind offered by RAND.

As disinvestment spread in the 1960s it led to a large increase in abandonment and fire. By the late-1960s vacant buildings, which accounted for only 0.5 percent of buildings in the city, accounted for 11 percent of structural fires and about 30 percent of multiple alarm fires. Abandoned buildings increased in number from an estimated 2,900 buildings in 1965 to 4,344 in 1969 – a 67 percent increase.[48]

An obvious way to deal with increasing fires is to hire more firefighters. Such was the conclusion of an arbitration board in January 1969. With the fire department's workload increased by 60 percent from 1964 to 1968 the firefighters' union wanted for workers in the next contract talks. In a chronicle well told by Joe Flood in *The Fires*, arbitrators agreed and appointed the "Flame Committee" to come up with solutions. The committee's solutions were clear: more firefighters and more backup companies, called "second sections" (companies at busy firehouses that go out when the first company is already engaged).

O'Hagan, not pleased with arbitrators and the union usurping his authority, asked RAND to come up with a counteroffer. RAND came up with a focus on false alarms. Using a firehouse in the Bronx as an example, Engine 82 made more than 6,000 runs in 1966. To relieve the company's workload, a second company, Engine 85, was added to the station with the expectation it would cut Engine 82's workload in half. It turned out Engine 82 remained the busiest firehouse in the city, with Engine 85 the second busiest, seemingly meaning no cut to the workload. False alarms were RAND's declared reason.

The problem was this was incomplete. When measuring actual fires the companies fought; putting aside false alarms which were a nuisance but not overly time consuming, Engine 82 dropped from the busiest in the city to fourth, with Engine 85 fifth – a reduced workload for Engine 82 as intended. Given that the number of fires in the area was rising, the secondary company was performing a much-needed service while relieving the first line company. This miscalculation was the nature of RAND's analysis for the duration of the partnership.

This first foray by RAND, in conjunction with O'Hagan, was

enough to get arbiters to pull back somewhat on the secondary stations and allow the department to mix in part-time tactical control units (TCUs) that operated to supplant companies during peak fire hours. While not as thorough as full-time companies the TCUs, along with the new secondary companies, were effective in reducing stress on the department.

Yet with budget issues flaring up, and an increasingly anti-union environment, Lindsay ordered a hiring freeze on uniform services in April 1971. As the number of firefighters reduced over time, O'Hagan was able to eliminate some of the secondary companies he never wanted. The TCU program would be canceled as volunteers serving in them requested transfers. Lindsay, now prepping for a White House run, ordered more cuts. RAND would come up with a plan.

It was a mess from the start. Moving companies to neighborhoods with more fires would obviously cut down on response times, thereby increasing efficiency. Of course, this would mean moving companies from wealthy and middle-class neighborhoods to poorer neighborhoods. Recognizing such an idea wasn't politically expedient, RAND divided the city's regions into seven "hazard categories" ("valuable commercial," "fireproof high-rise office," "large industrial with lumberyards and oil tanks," "high-density high fire-hazard residential," "lower-density less-hazardous residential," "mixed multi-story and one-or two-story frame," and "one-or tow-story frame") and compared neighborhoods only within each category. This led to the surreal dynamic of neighborhoods with low fire totals getting more service since they were compared only to other such neighborhoods while high fire neighborhoods lost service.

Add to this a flawed method in collecting response time data and faulty modeling[49], along with the seemingly inherent ability of analysts to talk themselves into anything, and New York was cutting fire service to poor neighborhoods with already worsening abandonment and fire problems – exactly the neighborhoods where the idea of planned shrinkage was bandied. The first cuts were announced in the fall of 1972; another wave came in 1975. That year the city cut 34 companies. By the time of the blackout the busiest companies were going on over 8,000 runs a year – 50 percent more than before the first round of cuts. The number of serious fires rose 40 percent from 1974 to 1977. Bushwick lost a secondary engine in 1972 (it lost a TCU the year before), the same for the Bronx.[50]

In the popular imagination, in keeping with the image of poor neighborhoods as lawless thunderdomes, arson was the primary cause of the fire epidemic. It certainly seems to be what Moynihan had in mind when he wrote in his memo, "Many of these fires are the result of population density. But a great many are more or less deliberately set." Or more poignantly later on when he said, as New York's senator in opposition to a proposed housing program in the Bronx, "People in the South Bronx don't want housing or they wouldn't burn it down. It's fairly clear that housing is not the problem in the South Bronx." In reality, during the 1950s, fire marshals in New York attributed less than 1 percent of fires to arson. The rate never got above 1.1 percent through 1975. While the rate increased in the late 1970s, as more buildings were abandoned, it never got over 7 percent.[51] The fire epidemic was a result of disinvestment, abandonment, and politics. From 1970 to 1980, New York lost 600,000 homes.

The neighborhoods most affected by the fire epidemic, including Harlem and the Lower East Side, have all now undergone at least some level of gentrification, many of them have basically been transformed. In the South Bronx, the Koch administration, to its credit, began a 10-year housing plan. By the mid-1980s federal funding for housing had declined further under the Reagan administration, about 70 percent from 1981-7. The city turned to public-private partnerships, investing billions to lend to nonprofits and developers. Once it gained steam in the late-1980s 100,000 units were renovated or constructed from

1987-93.[52] The good news is the Bronx has just about regained its population numbers from 1970 – between 1990 and 2013 the Bronx's population grew by 17 percent (faster than the city's 15 percent overall). The bad news: it took decades during which time the South Bronx remained the city's poorest and perhaps most stigmatized area.

In Bushwick the local community board and the Department of Housing Preservation and Development created the Bushwick Action Plan (endorsed by the Koch administration). This eventually led to the building of Hope Gardens, a low-rise public housing development (low-rise public housing fit the scale of Bushwick's two-family homes) on blocks that were emptied by fires. In what turned out to be the city's final large-scale public housing expansion, the city's housing authority built 1,076 low-income and 243 senior citizen housing units in Bushwick in the early to mid-1980s.[53]

Today Bushwick is rapidly filling with cafes, boutiques, and skyrocketing rents. The Rheingold Brewery, like the Domino site in Williamsburg, is being converted to high-end housing. Just as over a decade ago residents in Williamsburg put forward a community-based plan that was minimized by the city's government, Bushwick residents have put forward a plan to restrict large housing developments and preserve the neighborhood's existing industrial space that is getting similar treatment as a major rezoning hovers overhead.

It is not at all difficult to find apologists for the process that has been outlined here. After all, it was policy for decades and on the minds of planners long before then. A contingency can be seen from the 1929 RPA plan to the 1961 Zoning Law to Mayor Bloomberg's final State of the City address in February 2013 when he proclaimed: "From Long Island City and Hunters Point South to Greenpoint and Williamsburg and DUMBO, we have rezoned old industrial areas and brought them back to life."

Seen in this light gentrification can be a natural process.

Science writer Philip Ball, in *The Guardian* in 2014 under the title "Gentrification is a natural evolution," writes:

"Grumble all you like that Brixton's covered market, once called a '24-hour crack supermarket' by the local police, has been colonized by trendy boutique restaurants. The fact is that the gentrification of what was once an edgy part of London is almost a law of nature." The article posits, using research by Sergio Porta, that gentrification almost inevitably comes to neighborhoods some distance from the city center, with housing "typically dense but modest," and with a local street network that provides connection to the rest of the city while not disrupting the local feel of the neighborhood.[54]

If the process of gentrification is natural than resistance to it can be chalked up to simple, if understandable, nostalgia. Thus, Kay Hymowitz ends her book *The New Brooklyn: What it Takes to Bring a City Back* with this:

The longing to hold on to landscapes, streetscapes, and people of our youth is as human as mourning the dead...But it's worth remembering that people grieved the disappearance of fields and farmland when Brooklyn developers built the now-beloved, landmarked blocks of brownstones in the nineteenth century. They shuddered when factories replaced the fields along the waterfront – factories that people now fight to preserve. They fought when neighborhoods were cleared to build the treasured Brooklyn Bridge. Williamsburg's working class scowled when the artists arrived in the 1990s, while the artists cried foul when the Wall Streeters arrived in the new millennium...But Brooklyn and its proud residents have to understand the tension between their affection for their local history and both the needs of future city dwellers and the ephemerality of all things human...Bedford-Stuyvesant, to take just one example, goes from rural village to German bourgeois suburb to Jewish enclave to black ghetto to whatever comes next. Even Jane Jacobs wasn't born in the place she held up as a citified ideal. Nor, for that matter, did she die there. Like all of us she was just passing through.[55]

Of course all this is frivolous. Contrary to Ball's notion, there is nothing "natural" about the shape of cities; cities are obviously a product of politics, power, and struggle. Nostalgia is certainly a disease that infects every human mind and in ways that can be pointless or destructive, but regarding gentrification it is plainly a material, not nostalgic, matter.

In fairness, Hymowitz elsewhere acknowledges the vast inequality in Brooklyn and its cause. She writes:

The first requirement before the gentrifying middle-class moves into an area is, for better or worse, deindustrialization. The poor didn't have much choice in the matter...the middle class always preferred living at a distance from the toxic fumes, clanging machinery and trucks, foul smells...There was never going to be a mass middle-class homecoming to Brooklyn or any other city if it meant their kids would be growing up next to a sugar refinery[56].

Still to put this idea in its most positive light can go something like this: No divine entity sanctioned that factories operate on the Brooklyn waterfront. Factories were simply the most profitable investments for property owners at a particular time and place. The Brooklyn waterfront, as we know it, began as housing with views of the East River for the well-off, its return to housing with views of the East River for the well-off is just a natural economic process, not to mention an aesthetic improvement.

The main problem with this logic is its one-sidedness: only the alleged improvement is truly seen as natural. If reinvestment, or "development," is the shiny half of gentrification, then disinvestment and stigmentation are its dark counterparts, just as natural as the drip coffee cafes and organic shops. As stated earlier, it is this disinvestment (and requisite decline) that makes gentrification possible in the first place and – more to the point profitable for developers and politicians. Stigmentation allows for a revanchist mentally that certain neighborhoods must be rescued, by politicians and from its current inhabitants – such is why part of the Lower East Side is now called the "East Village" and in the early days of its gentrification, Bushwick was being dubbed "East Williamsburg."

The working class gets displacement and loss of community. Numerical studies about the numbers of displaced people in gentrifying neighborhoods are complex, to say the least, given the difficulty of getting exact data. A much lauded 2004 study by Lance Freeman and Frank Braconi, using data from the New York City Housing and Vacancy Survey, found that between 1996 and 1999 37,766 renters were displaced. They calculated this to be 5.47 percent of renters. Counterintuitively they found that poorer households in gentrifying areas were less likely to move than households in non-gentrifying areas thereby concluding that gentrification doesn't cause displacement, leading to such loud headlines as USA Today touting "Gentrification a boost for everyone" in 2005.[57]

Such findings were of course questioned. In 2006, Kathe Newman and Elvin K. Wyly offered a critique. Citing that many of the areas covered by the Freeman-Braconi study had fewer low-income residents left to begin with (and these households were covered by rent regulations) and the control group used poorer areas where large numbers of move could be expected, Newman and Wyly concluded that the Freeman-Braconi numbers were too low. Newman and Wyly estimate an annual range of displacement from 6.2 to 9.9 percent. In a city of over 8 million, this can still seem low in the grand scheme of things; bear in mind much of the displacement occurs in specific neighborhoods and it occurs every year. Over a period of a few years that spells large changes in these neighborhoods.[58]

In an influential study back in 1985, Peter Marcuse identified additional types of displacement beyond direct displacement. These included "chain displacement," households that may have been forced to move at an earlier point in a building's decline, and "exclusionary displacement" which occurs when a housing unit is gentrified or abandoned so that a similar household (income wise) is prevented from moving into the unit. Then there is the fact that displacement certainly affects others living in a gentrifying environment. As Marcuse wrote:

When a family sees the neighborhood around it changing dramatically, when their friends are leaving the neighborhood, when the stores they patronize are liquidating and new stores for other clientele are taking their places, and when changes in public facilities, in transportation patterns, and in support services all clearly are making the area less and less livable... Families living under these conditions may move as soon as they can, rather than wait for the inevitable: nonetheless they are displaced.[59]

Still the apologist can correctly exclaim, "neighborhoods in New York are always changing, have always changed, and change is inevitable. If gentrification is synonymous with neighborhoods becoming wealthier and whiter and minorities being displaced New York is still really diverse. After all the Hispanic population in North Brooklyn may be declining but the Hispanic, as well as Asian population, in the overall city is climbing."

While obviously true this overlooks the fact that much of the historic neighborhood change wasn't due to gentrification. Another caveat to that logic is the case of African-Americans. As historically black neighborhoods such as Harlem, Bedford-Stuyvescent have gentrified, the city's black population has declined. From 2000-10 the city's black population declined 5.1

percent, as from 28 percent of the city's population to 22.8. This is hardly limited to New York; black populations have been declining in North Eastern cities across the board. However, given the unique history of African-American struggle in the US, the transformation of neighborhoods like Harlem can be said to deserve special attention.

Harlem certainly goes back a long way. The name comes from the Dutch "Haarlem" back in the city's New Amsterdam days. Harlem has served as a refuge to many groups over time: Germans, Jews, Irish. For a time it was New York's largest "Little Italy." East Harlem has long been known as "El Barrio," for a period New York's signature Puerto Rican and Dominican neighborhood (certainly a great deal of flux but, again, not gentrification). Yet the very mention of Harlem immediately brings to mind its long history as an African-American neighborhood. From the Harlem Renaissance of the 1920s through years of disinvestment and stigmentation, Harlem was a major center of African-American culture. As local historian Michael Henry Adams put it:

Harlem has lovely old buildings reflecting varied cultures, even former synagogues. But throughout history, nothing about Harlem has made it renown, worldwide, apart from black people. One may talk all one likes about other earlier Harlems populated by people who were not black. By contrast, these white Harlems were insignificant. African Americans alone – our culture, drive, and creativity – have accorded a status as fabled and fabulous as that held by Paris or Rome.

Still seen from a macro point of view perhaps lamenting the loss of any particular neighborhood misses the greater point. The greater point is the movement of capital, what Neil Smith described as a "see-saw" movement. The development of the rent gap, which again depends on the withdrawal of capital and subsequent decline, was due to the vast project of suburbanization that occurred in the midst of a severe housing shortage after World War II.

It is true that a pattern of suburbanization existed long before the New Deal. There was an American uniqueness that saw wealthier people moving away from the central core of cities, at the time the opposite of European cities like Paris, Vienna, and Berlin. In Crabgrass Frontier: The Suburbanization of the United States, Kenneth Jackson argues that if not for annexation movement by cities in the nineteenth century (most famously the 1898 consolidation of New York City into the present five boroughs and Philadelphia's large expansion), suburbanization would have set in even sooner.

This still doesn't mean that the post-war explosion was inevitable. In Picture Windows: How the Suburbs Happened Rosalyn Baxandall and Elizabeth Ewan cite a 1946 Fortune survey that revealed: "The US people are strikingly in favor of positive government action to end the severe housing shortage. A majority of those with opinions want the government to embark on a large scale building program," and that more people, particularly the young, veterans, the poor, and those living in large cities, and especially in North Atlantic states, i.e. most people, preferred renting an apartment to owning a home. The Economic Report of the President to the Congress in 1949 stated that "about 80% of the housing now being built is for sale, although veterans and others with families of uncertain future size and jobs of uncertain tenure would much prefer to rent."

Given the uncertainty and even preference for renting and city life why weren't more rentals built and instead home ownership elevated to the center of American culture? As Picture Windows puts it:

> The answer is that Levitt, Burns, Lustrom, and the other master Builders, along with their allies – the bank and loan associations, real Estate lobby, lumber industry, media,

chambers of commerce, and Conservative politicians –
knew rental housing would never make them money. The
automobile industry, the highway lobby, and other appliance
manufactures felt the same way. Together these groups tried
to persuade the government and the public that individual
home ownership was crucial for preserving "the American
way of life."[60]

Simply put, profit rates in the suburbs were higher and in an
important sense for reasons that would later bring gentrification
to cities. Land was open and available and ground rent was
low, making building in the suburbs cheaper than building
in already existing cities. This was especially so given the
vast government subsidies. In 1934 the FHA was created. The
FHA induced and insured loans, mostly by insuring a higher
percentage of individual loans and thus allowing lower down
payments. Interest rates fell due to lower risk and default. The
FHA also established minimum standards for construction and
extended the pay period for its guaranteed mortgages to up to
30 years. Crucially, at the same time the FHA adopted HOLC's
neighborhood classifications greatly expanding redlining. By the
early 1970s the FHA assisted around 11 million families to own
homes and 22 million homeowners to improve their property.

The 1956 Interstate Highway Act provided funding for
42,500 miles of freeway, with the Federal government paying
90 percent of the cost. Between 1950 and 1970 the suburban
population doubled, accounting for 83 percent of total growth
in the country. While large pockets of cities were redlined
under FHA guidelines, the suburbs were subsidized. The New
York area gives an insight into how this played out. From the
mid-1940s to the mid-1970s, Nassau County, a single suburban
county on Long Island, received more home loans than all of the
city combined (162,669 to 146,691). Next-door Suffolk County
received 76,543 loans while the Bronx got 9927. To the north of

the Bronx, suburban Westchester received nearly three times that amount (29,660).

However, in the present day, a 2017 report from the Long Island Association states that poverty in Long Island is at its highest level since 1959. A study done the year before by United Way of New York found that 35 percent of Long Island households fall into the category of "ALICE" – Asset Limited Income Strained, Employed, meaning these households have a difficult time meeting their regular expenses.

Today as city cores become wealthier, now mirroring the European pattern, poverty in the suburbs has increased (hence the see-saw). Since 2000 suburbia has experienced sharper increases in poverty than urban areas. From 2000-15 suburbs in the country's largest metro areas saw the numbers of residents living below the poverty line grow by 57 percent. It is part of what Alan Ehrenhalt calls a "demographic inversion."[61] While the national poverty rates in urban and rural areas remain greater than in suburban areas, the suburbs have grown poorer and more diverse as many gentrified urban areas have done the opposite (for instance much of the attention on the street gang MS-13 is diverted hysteria about Hispanic immigration yet it is worth pointing out that this is taking place largely in Long Island, not New York City).

The shift is due to many of the same factors that have contributed to poverty everywhere: deindustrialization, a low-wage economy, immigration to suburban areas, yet it is also due to the way capital moves. Investment in one area leads to potential profits lessening the more an area develops, meanwhile previously forsaken areas gain in potential. Just as the suburbs presented a higher rate of return given their once open land, thereby creating decline and rent-gaps in cities, these rent-gaps along with development of the suburbs inevitably becoming less profitable as those early factors lessened, make central cities more profitable luring capital to swing back. This makes gentrification "therefore the product not simply of capitalist organization of space but the specific needs of capital at a given time, and it is here that we must broaden our focus...at the entire transformation of central cities."[62]

An age of gentrification hasn't reduced poverty in New York. It has increased poverty in the city as well as simply shifting poverty outside the city. Frederick Engels writing in The Housing Question way back in 1872 had a clear vision of this:

> By "Haussmann" I mean the practice which has now become general of making breaches in the working class quarters of our big towns, and particularly in those which are centrally situated, quite apart from whether this is done from considerations of public health and for beautifying the town, or owing to the demand for big centrally situated business premises...No matter how different the reasons may be, the result is everywhere the same: the scandalous alleys and lanes disappear to the accompaniment of lavish self-praise from the bourgeoisie on account of this tremendous success, but they appear again immediately somewhere else often in the immediate neighborhood.

For cities this presents what geographer Tom Slater labels "false choice urbanism," between gentrification (reinvestment) and ghettoization (disinvestment). With this false choice urbanism uneven development is a given, every city is either rising or declining. The idea that such a system is natural is indeed reactionary. As Slater writes: "The implications are disturbing – it is only a short leap from saying that gentrification is a natural evolution to saying that austerity is a natural evolution, tax evasion is a natural evolution, rentier capitalism is a natural evolution."[63]

Central to the process is an obvious lack of community control (for instance City Hall's all but discarding of community board plans) both in housing and the workplace – the latter is too often overlooked. In 1968 philosopher Henri Lefebvre put forward the idea of "The Right to the City." Lefebvre's "cry and demand" can appear fuzzy, yet he was clear in a 1989 essay "Quand la ville se perd une metamorphose planetaire," writing "the right to the city implies nothing less than a revolutionary conception of citizenship." In an earlier book titled Metaphilosophy, Lefebvre posited what he called "precious residues" – philosophical after-thoughts. In an urban context the residues are the displaced, the low-wage workers, the homeless. Andy Merrifield puts it thusly:

> The right to the city is now about those who have been expelled – the residues – reclaiming, or claiming for the first time, their right to a collective urban life, to an urban society they're actively making yet are hitherto disenfranchised from.[64]

Chapter 2

Spend enough time with the tedious New York tabloids, listening to talk radio, or reading conservative punditry, and before long one is bound to come across the words "bad old days" where the subject is New York City. The phrase has been uttered or written so many times it becomes difficult to know exactly to which days a writer is referring. A close reading suggests these days generally fall into two categories.

There's the late 1980s to the early 1990s, the height of the national crack epidemic, when like cities across the country New York was engulfed in a high murder rate. The narrative here is of a city rescued from chaos by the election of the heroic Rudy Giuliani who, along with his innovative Police Commissioner Bill Bratton employing the forward thinking strategies of Compstat and "broken windows" policing, made New York the safest big city in America (Bratton would be forced out when Giuliani deemed Bratton was drawing too much of the spotlight. Giuliani would have two other police commissioners, the last of which, Bernard Kerik, would go on to be convicted of tax fraud and making false statements a few years after his term as commissioner. Even official stories have their warts).

It is not difficult to puncture this mythology. The drop in crime began under David Dinkins and his Safe Streets, Safe City program that added more police to the streets. Dinkins' final commissioner, Ray Kelly, who would be reappointed to commissioner for Michael Bloomberg's three terms as mayor and implement the ultra-draconian stop-and-frisk policy, wrote in his recent book *Vigilance: My Life Serving America and Protecting Its Empire City*, "The Giuliani administration had only to pass out the uniforms and send the new recruits onto the street. It was the Dinkins administration that handed Giuliani and Police Commissioner Bill Bratton the single most valuable tool for turning campaign rhetoric into practical policy." Like the rise in crime, the drop in crime in New York mirrored the drop in crime nationally (albeit New York's was larger). It's also well worth noting that despite its sensationalized reputation New York was never the country's most crime-ridden city. In fact, in 1993 New York ranked 88th in crime out of 183 municipalities with 100,000 or more people[1]. New York's reputation stemmed from its national prominence and its standing as a media headquarters. Cities such as Chicago, Detroit, and St Louis didn't feature Paul Kersey and Travis Bickle blowing away their criminal classes. Martin Scorsese's early days as a director saw him make his most brilliant films but he certainly didn't burnish New York's reputation.

Mean Streets and *Taxi Driver* bring us to the other period often characterized as the "bad old days," the mid-to-late 1970s. The context here is not first and foremost crime and paranoia, though those certainly factor in, but economic bankruptcy and abandonment. Indeed it was certainly a bleak time. Proof of that can be discerned from the enduring legacy of two of the city's cultural treasures that had their roots during the crisis: the "I Love NY" campaign of 1977 which originated with the New York State Department of Commerce and Mark Donnelly, Art Director for New York State, hiring the Well Rich Greene agency and graphic designer Milton Glaser for a marketing campaign to energize New York tourism, and Frank Sinatra's 1980 recording of "Theme from New York, New York" (*New York New York* the film was Scorsese's 1970s flop featuring Liza Minnelli's original version of the Theme song that would be reduced to an afterthought). Both clearly speak for a city directly and indirectly yearning to boost its spirit and economy (while a constant staple at cheesy tourist shops, Glaser's "I Love NY" logo would find particular renewed enthusiasm in the weeks after the 9/11 attacks).

The narrative of the 1970s crisis goes like this: New York was plunged into bankruptcy by overspending – that is overspending on such ignoble things as welfare, overly generous salaries and pensions for city workers, and free City College. This led to the city's bonds being cut off by banks, the establishment of the Emergency Financial Control Board to oversee the city's finances, in other words to cut spending (and reducing elected officials to basically nonentities), the eventual election of Ed Koch to at least initially continue the austerity and restore the city finances leading to the Wall Street boom of the 1980s (Koch's terms coming in the pre-Fox News era, and being a Democrat, though no enemy of conservatism and though credited as such, he misses out on the lionization that Giuliani has basked in).

The obvious common thread that ties these dark periods together is the triumphal assertion of conservatism, in both its tough law-and-order and economic form, to rescue a city hovering on the brink. The line not only serves as a lesson in history but is useful as a bulwark against any subsequent progressive alternatives which could be hauntingly declared by their opponents to harken back to the given "bad old days."

Much like the 1990s drop in crime the defenses for this narrative can be penetrated. The very basic problem did boil down to New York not being able to sell its bonds. Years of short-term borrowing for long-term expenses and budgeting gimmicks ballooned debt. Bonds are basically debt securities whereby buyers are effectively lending money to the issuer by purchasing the bond. In exchange the issuer, in this case a city, promises to pay regular interest payments to the bond holder, often every 6 months, and then ultimately return the original investment (i.e. the cost of the bond, known as the principal) at the bond maturity date usually years into the future depending on whether the bond is short or long-term. The main kinds of short-term debt New York issued at the time were tax anticipation notes (TANs), most often issued against unpaid real estate assessments, revenue anticipation notes (RANs), issued against earned but uncollected federal and state aid, and bond anticipation notes (BANs) against approved debt issues (bonds are issued by governments against specific future revenues to give buyers the confidence of knowing where their repayment is coming from).

The problem was the revenues weren't showing up. Given that the city was losing population, with many properties simply being abandoned, tax proceeds were overestimated. The overestimates were used to justify issuing TANs and when the tax money didn't show up the city would simply roll them over by issuing new TANs. The same dynamic was in play for RANs. As the city sought more federal aid that increasingly wasn't coming (Nixon's election, OPEC embargo) the issuing of RANs increased topping a billion dollars in 1971.

By mid-1974 the city's debt was $11 billion, $3.4 billion of which was in short-term notes. Over 11 percent of the city's spending went to debt service. Then Mayor Beame transferred $750 million in expenditures into the capital budget while the city needed to borrow about 5 billion from late 1974 to early 1975 (the capital budget is meant to be a separate budget for long-term physical improvement projects such as schools, libraries, sewers, etc. This budget trick went back a few years. In the mid-1960s the city used $7 million from the capital budget this way). Large commercial banks started discreetly selling off some of their New York holdings. In order to stimulate the bond market, the city reduced denominations from $25,000 to $10,000 and underwriters kept increasing the interest rates. In July 1974 Comptroller Harrison Golden called the 7.92 percent interest rates the banks were demanding an "unconscionable cost"; a week later the city paid 8.58 percent. Banks demanded austerity. An October bond issue went poorly, and by April 1975 it reached a point where the city's bond market dried up (with the banks unloading and flooding the market) pushing the city to the brink of default and bankruptcy since it lacked the funds it needed for payments on what it already owed. In May 1975 then New York State Governor Hugh Carey, working in conjunction with various business leaders, created the MAC to issue new bonds (administered by the state but guaranteed by city taxes). By July MAC bonds were also not selling well prompting further calls for austerity, from June to December 1975 40,000 city workers were laid off.

In October Governor Carey established the Emergency Financial Control Board (EFCB) to oversee city spending – the board would have Mayor Beame as a member but by now his power, and thereby democratic control, was severely curtailed. EFCB established some discipline, refusing to accept a negotiated contract with the city's teachers union (UFT), but couldn't reopen the bond market forcing the city to look to Washington for financial support. Despite the appeal not only from New York but mayors of 15 cities, on October 29 at the National Press Club, Gerald Ford gave a speech announcing that he was prepared to veto any bill that would amount to a federal bailout of New York. The next day the *New York Daily News* ran the most infamous headline in the city's history: FORD TO CITY: DROP DEAD.

From there the UFT would invest $150 million of its pension fund into city bonds, the federal government would somewhat reverse its tough stand in November and provide the city with key seasonal loans, the contentious 1977 mayoral election would see the emergence of Ed Koch, the election took place a few months after the two night blackout in July and related rioting and only weeks from the large Bronx fire being a story in Game 2 of the World Series – events which greatly assisted his election. Koch would impose further austerity and the city would allegedly rebound on the back of the Manhattan real estate boom and the go-go 80s bull market on Wall Street.

All in all New York had needed to come up with $6.8 billion in financing to cover from the end of 1975 through June 1978 by which time, according to the bill that created the EFCB, the city was expected to achieve a balanced budget. With the federal government's $2.3 billion in seasonal loans providing stability, the city's unions purchased $2.5 billion in debt with their pension funds while also agreeing to forgo interest payments and reinvest the money in city bonds; MAC owners agreed to bonds with lower interest rates and longer terms on payback, the state advanced $800 million, new taxes took in $500 million, and banks rolled over a $1 billion in debt.

An obvious question hangs over the crisis. Even in his callous October speech Ford raised the important point. Here's a quote from the speech:

> Many explanations have been offered about what led New York City deeper and deeper into this quagmire. Some contend it was long term economic forces such as the flight to the suburbs of the city's more affluent citizens, the migration to the city of poor people, and the departure of industry. Others argued that the big Metropolitan city has become obsolescent...and New York's downfall could not be prevented. Let's face one simple fact: most other cities in America have faced these very same challenges and they are still financially healthy today. They have not been luckier than New York, they've simply been better managed.

It is well worth looking at every explanation cited by Ford in his speech. The early 1970s aren't considered a golden age for cities, especially older cities on the East Coast and Rust Belt. There was a national economic downturn and OPEC's oil embargo hit the northeast harder than the expanding Sun Belt since it imported more oil. Cold War spending favored newer cities and a warmer climate (for instance, San Diego ranks at least near the top of numerous lists of American cities for living and visiting for its natural beauty, climate, location, etc. It is also, however, perhaps the most militarized metropolitan area in the world). Cold War theory favored suburbs due to their more dispersed populations. In the event of nuclear war, the less population density per square mile apparently means less death per missile strike.

When Richard Nixon was elected, federal aid to cities declined, the then almost all-white suburbs being the Republican base and thus more worthy recipients. The anti-city bias of the federal government would continue for years to come, with all the inherent racial politics. In the first pages of his book *The Assassination of New York*, Robert Fisk quotes one of the MAC people's answer to Fitch's question about the causes of the crisis: "It's the fucking blacks and Puerto Ricans."

Still for all that, the fact remains that many American cities endured all of the above yet it was New York that entered a financial abyss. So what separated New York? In the book *Political Crisis/Fiscal Crisis: The Collapse and Revival of New York City*, Martin Shefter makes the interesting point that the financial crisis of 1975 should be seen in the context of other such crises that erupted periodically in New York's history. Shefter cites the crises of 1856, 1871, 1914, 1932-33, in addition to the one of 1975. The pattern in all these was a city unable to sell its bonds and facing the possibility of not paying its creditors or employees. In most instances after agreeing to stiff financial concessions the city was bailed out by banks or higher government after which, in all but one case, an incumbent mayor was driven from power by a "fusion" candidate claiming the banner of reform.

The standard answer from conservatives is New York let social welfare and such spending get out of control to the point that it bankrupted the city. Spending in this context obviously would entail programs associated with progressive politics. A good place to start is with the greatest progressive boogieman in conservative mythology: public assistance, particularly in the form of the old AFDC (Aid to Families with Dependent

Children). It is true that New York spent a large amount of welfare and that welfare roll rose considerably in the 1960s, growing 32 percent a year from 1966 to 1970. However in the following years, 1971-75, rolls grew at a much lesser pace of 6.9 percent.

There are two contextual factors that must be noted. First, the surge in the public assistance enrollment in New York in the 1960s stemmed from rolls being kept artificially low in the 1950s by arbitrary and discriminating administration (New York State's rolls grew more in the early 1970s than New York City's did).

A further issue is that funding that the city was required to pick up by the state was higher in New York than the national average. No state mandated as heavy a share of public assistance costs on its local municipalities as New York (this would become particularly important when it came to Medicaid costs where the same dynamic existed). Actually 43 states and territories participating in federal programs covered the entirety of the costs. The cost of living in New York also mandated higher funding but overall New York was by no means unique. In 1974 New York ranked sixth in the percentage of public assistance recipients behind Boston (16.9 percent), Baltimore (16.3 percent), Philadelphia (16.2), St Louis (15.8), and Newark (14.4). The city's ranking was even comparable in welfare fraud, something that really makes the conservative blood boil. Actual public assistance payments – $94 per month in 1974 – were lower than those in Chicago, Philadelphia, or Milwaukee. Inflated public assistance rolls didn't account for New York's financial crisis[2].

Neither did public sector workers, the other villain of the conservative universe (indeed in a post-welfare world, public sector workers, with their high rates of unionization, are probably the main enemies). New York's municipal workforce grew by 46.7 percent from 1961 to 1971 but this was basically half of 89 percent of state and local growth across the country. Like the public assistance rolls, the public workforce cost grew by a higher rate in the late 1960s, 18 percent a year from 1966 to 1970, than it did in the early 1970s (9.7 percent). According to figures listed in Charles R. Morris' book *The Cost of Good Intentions: New York City and the Liberal Experiment* (a book that by its title alone can be said to not be overly sympathetic to liberalism) the increase in per capita expenditure for municipal functions from 1965-66 to 1973-74 in New York (68.8 percent) was less than DC (81.8), Baltimore (150), Detroit (121.4), Cleveland (101), and Chicago (87.4). Morris notes regarding New York during the Lindsay years: "...changes in employee compensation appear to be not much different than those found anywhere else. The causes of the disproportionate increase in city costs will have to be sought elsewhere."[3]

Two areas of spending that were more unique to New York were the city's public hospitals and universities (the university system known as CUNY). Since its inception CUNY offered a free college education to working-class New York. Due to adopting open enrollment in 1970 CUNY, as well as the state system (SUNY), underwent an expansion; however, echoing previously discussed spending, enrollment and staff growth at CUNY grew faster in the 1960s. Overall the cost of CUNY was considerable (for what should be an obviously worthy cause, half the cost at the time was assumed by the city), growing at twice the rate of the city budget but in 1975 it still only made up 4.6 percent of the city's expense budget – certainly not enough to trigger the financial crisis.

No city in the country has a public hospital system the size of New York's. At its peak size New York ran two dozen hospitals along with dozens of clinics. While the system sustained problems of inefficiency and funding that lowered the quality of care as time went on, it provided healthcare to millions of people every year particularly in poor neighborhoods, as well as a source of employment. However, with the establishment of Medicaid in 1965, even though state law required the city pay 25 percent of the cost – a cost requirement that no other big city in the country faced, the growth rate of expenditures for the municipal hospital system declined. A 1977 report by the Temporary Commission on City Finances showed that from 1961-76 tax-levy expenditures for city hospitals grew by 150 percent. If this sounds like a lot it is significantly less than the increase over the same period for the police and fire departments and education and just about equal to sanitation.

If the role of social spending in the crisis has been exaggerated then what were the most immediate causes of the crisis? To begin with, the explosion in the contract, supplies, and equipment line of the budget should be pointed out. That line grew by 620 percent from 1961 to 1975, twice the rate of the overall expense budget and faster than the much-maligned workforce that used the purchased supplies. By 1975 the cost amounted to $1.3 billion, 11 percent of the total budget and two-and-a-half times more than CUNY[4]. This rise was partially due to increased use of outside consultants by then Mayor Lindsay, including the destructive RAND partnership, and probably to a combination of inefficient and political contracting and purchasing.

It's also vital to note that the city's spending was mirrored, indeed surpassed, by the state. It was the era of Governor Nelson Rockefeller who reigned from 1959 to 1973 (his brother David was conveniently head of Chase Manhattan Bank at the same time). Under his watch New York spent more than any other state. The budget increased from $2.04 billion in 1960 to $8.8 billion in 1974.[5] As for debt that grew from $1.97 billion in 1961 to $13.37 billion in 1973, again the largest in the nation. The Rockefeller fingerprints are spread all over post-industrial New York. Rockefeller Center, the original World Trade Center, Battery Park City, Lincoln Center, the South Street Seaport, the United Nations; they are all directly tied to Rockefeller money and power.

Like the city, the state funded much of its spending with bonds. The thing is that New York's state constitution requires voter approval for the issuing of general obligation bonds. Governor Rockefeller cannily got around that hindrance by creating public authorities that could borrow and spend without approval of voters or the legislature. Using what were called "moral obligation bonds," a clever trickery devised by John Mitchell, who would later achieve notoriety and jail time as Nixon's Attorney General during Watergate, these bonds were not backed by the full credit of the state but with the expectation that the legislature would support them (but there was no "legal" obligation to do so), the state turned into a cash cow. By 1974 New York had almost a quarter of all the outstanding nonguaranteed long-term debt in the US. Most prominent of the 230 public authorities that Rockefeller created was the Urban Development Corporation (UDC). Established in 1968 UDC's main function was to build housing; Roosevelt Island in New York City was UDC's biggest project, and it had the power of eminent domain along with the power to override local zoning laws. The well dried up in February 1974 when UDC defaulted on repayment of $104.5 million worth of notes. Though the state, by now under Governor Hugh Carey (with Rockefeller gone along with his shenanigans), came up with the money a few weeks later the fallout affected the city's bond market.

The state's harebrained mechanics gave the city the tools to follow it off the cliff. At the time of the UDC default much of the city's short-term debt was wrapped up in financing mortgages. The late 1960s, a time of economic prosperity, featured the largest building boom on office space in New York's history. As deindustrialization increased, jobs in offices at first made up for the loss of industry. The ensuing national downturn, along with the globalization of banking, hit New York harder than other cities given the prominence of financial industry.

While handing out tax abatements to developers is often

declared standard operating procedure for cities, it should be pointed out that with manufacturing on the decline the city was leaning heavily on white collar jobs that would fill up the many new office buildings. The sheer scale of construction, 7 million to 14 million square feet worth of office space, was built every year from 1967-70, 66.7 million square feet from 1967 to 1973. This was hardly the work of the free market. The reason for granting tax abatements was precisely because the market wouldn't support the construction. When the inevitable downturn came in the early 1970s the city was left with an ocean of empty space. The World Trade Center, opened in 1973, itself added 9 million square feet of office space the city didn't need. The subsidizing of office space led to higher land values motivating the city government again to inject itself into subsidizing more development as housing developers and related industries were eager for it. The state may have invented BAN financing but it was the city that took it to a new level with its massive financing of the Mitchell-Lama housing program. This was the first program to openly provide government philanthropy for the middle class. In return for some limits on profits, developers could receive mortgages from the city or state for 90 percent of project costs at lower interest rates than the private market provided, along with property tax exemptions.[6] The $3 billion the city threw into mortgages was about a third of its debt. This wasn't for public housing for poorer people. This was for middle-income housing mortgages. By 1969 more than 57,000 Mitchell-Lama apartments had been built in New York, most occupied by upper-middle class tenants. In total 139,000 such apartments were built.

In his book *The Rise and Fall of New York City*, Roger Starr, the city's housing commissioner until he was forced to resign when he publicly endorsed the nasty concept of "planned shrinkage," writes of the city's housing funding:

If, indeed, there had been no fiscal crisis, the worthless

Housing debt would have been greater, probably much greater. The only thing that kept the moderate-income housing program from continuing forever was the crisis itself. Residents liked it (until their rents rose, though not nearly enough to cover costs). Builders liked it, because they made money on land and construction. The building trade unions liked it, because it kept them busy. The financial World liked it, because they could buy city obligations which are, effectively, guaranteed by taxpayers as well as residents.[7]

Or as Fitch puts it more succinctly in *The Assassination of New York:*

But New York borrowed not just to pay expenses, until revenues arrived, but to make mortgages. No other city borrowed even a dollar for this purpose. New York borrowed more than $3 billion...The state and city were in a kind of competition to see who could please their number one political constituency – the city's finance, insurance and real estate (FIRE) industry.[8]

The scale of overall tax exemptions was vast. Despite the building boom, or indeed because of it, real estate tax dropped from 42 percent of total revenues in 1961 to 24 percent in 1975. There was no real estate slump, values doubled from 1960 to 1971. Two factors accounted for the decline of relative revenue: outright exemptions and drops in assessment. The real estate that was completely exempt from taxation stood at 28 percent in the mid-1950s. However, with those Rockefeller projects like Battery Park City and the World Trade Center – the latter cost $700 million in lost taxes by 1979, by 1976 the number was up to 40 percent. As for assessments, overall assessments values dropped from 82.2 percent of market value in 1960-61 to only 48 percent of market value in 1975.[9] Homes outside of Manhattan have always been assessed at a lower rate than commercial or industrial homes and less frequently meaning that the lower assessments here came from Central Business District in Midtown (home of much of the subsidized office construction). In 1972, property taxes overall accounted for slightly over half of New York's total local revenue compared to roughly 80 percent for the rest of the country's 20 largest cities. All the subsidized development bled New York of revenue that likely would have prevented the crisis.

Of course there was also the behavior of the banks. By late 1974, in the aftermath of UDC's default, internal memos show that the banks had knowledge of a pending crisis. Yet a December $400 million bond offering with a 9.4 percent interest rate and including low denominations of $10,000, sold well as did a $620 million offering on January 7, 1975. The success of the offerings testifies to one of two alternatives: either the city's finances were not in bad shape, or investors who purchased the bonds didn't know the full extent of the problem. Foreshadowing the crisis of 2008, the major rating agencies, Moody's and Standard & Poor, actually upgraded New York's bonds from the Baa rating they had given since 1965, to a more enticing A rating in 1972 and 1973. Moody's A rating would last well into 1975, probably on the basis that New York, like twenty-first century banks, was too big to fail. Here it is the time to point out that from the summer of 1974 through March 1975 the big banks dumped $2.3 billion of their own New York securities holdings on the market pushing the bond market over edge. A SEC report from the time spells it out:

As the City's fiscal crisis worsened, the public was subjected to a confusing and contradictory financial picture with the result that the public, unlike the City and its underwriters, was deprived of a basic understanding of the City's finances.

While the public was left largely uniformed, the City's underwriters had an increasing awareness of the range of problems underlying the City's fiscal crisis. During 1974 and 1975, certain of the underwriters of City securities ceased purchasing City securities for their fiduciary accounts. Despite the shift of investment policy, they continued as underwriters to market these securities to the public. The underwriters did not disclose this significant change in their investment strategy and policy.

It was during this period that bankers' thinking drifted globally. OPEC's embargo may have been a prime factor in the stagnation of the 1970s but it was a bonanza for banks. Petrodollars earned from higher oil prices flowed into American banks where they were turned into loans to the developing world. Latin American countries would borrow about $200 billion from 1970 to 1981.[10] Citibank, for one, expanded its international business from $6 billion in 1970 to $28.7 billion in 1974. The global expansion, along with laws passed in the 1960s allowing banks to create Real Estate Investment Trusts, gave banks less incentive to purchase municipal bonds. When the real estate market dried up in the early 1970s leaving the banks with bad debt it would drive them even further to seek global profit.

A summary of the banks' part in the crisis amounts to: encouraging and underwriting the city's debt, covertly dumping their holdings of that debt at the sign of trouble thereby flooding the market and hurting the city while duping investors, continuing to underwrite bonds while doing so, and then, rather than acknowledging their role in the crisis and working with the city's government when the market dried up, demanding austerity. The ironic tragedy is the banking industry was able to gain more control of New York's economy while actually divesting in the city, not investing.

If different forms of corporate welfare and poor urban

planning were at least as responsible as social spending for the financial crisis, if not the main causes, the practical results of the crisis fell squarely on those at the bottom rather than the top. Tuition was charged at CUNY for the first time. In the current age of tuition bubbles and Democratic politicians promoting plans on making college cheaper it is difficult to grasp what a major break this was at the time. CUNY had been free for over a century. Despite pressure from the governor five members of the Board of Education resigned rather than vote for establishing tuition charges.

The poverty rate in the Bronx rose from 19.5 percent in 1970 to 27.6 percent in 1980. In Brooklyn the rate jumped from 17.6 percent to 24 percent. A total of 15,000 teachers and paraprofessionals, 20 percent of the union membership, was laid off in 1975. The number of police officers was cut by 13.7 percent. By 1980 there were 5000 less sanitation worker jobs and less frequent street sweeping. Only about half of the city's streets were acceptably clean at the time.

Parks and playground declined from underfunding and didn't rebound for a decade. Their eventual rebound involved partnerships with nonprofits and corporations, known as conservatories, which, while making obvious aesthetic improvements, raises questions about the privatization of public space. Admission to Central Park Zoo was once free. Under the management of the Wildlife Conservation Society (WCS) since 1980, "total experience" tickets now cost $19.95 for adults (people aged 12 and up) and $14.95 for children (general admission $13.95 for adults and $9.95 for children). The Bronx Zoo, also managed by WCS, boasts "total experience" ticket prices of $36.95 for adults, $26.95 for children, and $31.95 for seniors. New York Aquarium in Coney Island: $29.95 for adults, $24.95 for children.

However, beyond all the closed clinics and dirtier streets and parks, the greatest legacy of the financial crisis has been the lasting conservative hegemony it established over the city's economic policy. For many in power this was the point all along. The EFCB dropped the "emergency" in 1986 when it ceased having formal approval over the city's budget – 1986 was the year the city repaid the federal government the last of the more than $1 billion it borrowed; however the board still exists as the Financial Control Board (FCB). While it serves as a review board, by law its approval power would be restored if the city ran a deficit of more than $100 million.

When it became clear by April 1975, after another round of budget cuts, Major Beame would label them "murderous," including closing public research libraries on Saturdays, eliminating subsidies to nursing schools, and proposals to shrink the city's workforce by 10 percent and cutting CUNY by $70 million (students occupied the dean's office at Hunter College), that the city's bond market wasn't reopening and it would need federal assistance, the city ran smack into the Ford Administration.

Ford himself years later would wrongly say regarding New York's crisis, "the problem was New York had a bad policy of paying too much in pensions, paying too much in salaries to New York City employees. And the city was going bankrupt because of this irresponsible fiscal policy[11]." His administration featured a cast of characters including Treasury Secretary William Simon, whose department included Arthur Laffer, soon to be recognized as the father of supply side economics through the bogus Laffer Curve, Chief of Staff Donald Rumsfeld (later Ford's Secretary of Defense), and a young Randian named Alan Greenspan.

It was the time of the Southern Strategy and conservative backlash and it went beyond Washington. In June 1975 the *New York Times* published an article featuring 18 urban experts to "Advise, Castrate, and Console the City on its Problems." While the term "urban experts" was perhaps used a little too

71

loosely, the list did feature the likes of Jane Jacobs and Lewis Mumford. A few advisors advocated New York receive federal help. The social democrat Michael Harrington wrote: "By the passage of three laws in Washington, you could end the crisis immediately," also stating "catching up with all the other advanced industrial democracies (through a national system of health care) and achieving full employment." Robert C. Wood, then professor at the University of Massachusetts and former director of the Joint Center of Urban Studies wrote: "The idea that playing around with tuition at CUNY, and trying to lay off policemen and firemen, and tricks in rolling over short-term notes, will somehow solve the problem is fallacious. There have to be massive infusions of national and state money because cities happen to be national and state assets."

Yet the overall sentiment of the *Times'* chorus went the other way. Milton Friedman, fresh off of advising the Pinochet regime in Chile, suggested the city:

Go bankrupt. That will make it impossible for New York City in future to borrow any money and force New York to live within its budget. The only other alternative is the obvious one – tighten its belt, pay off its debt, live within its means, and become an honest city again. That's a much better solution from the long-run point of view, but whether it's a politically feasible solution I don't know, whereas the first one is.

Roy Wilkins, head of the NAACP, claimed: "What New York needs in common with most cities of over 25,000 population is a reduction in the number of municipal employees. The scale of salaries and pensions here is higher than elsewhere because living is more expensive than in any other city in America." Herbert Stein, former chairman of President's Council of Economic Advisers, wrote: "I think that the prescription of New

York cutting down its services, cutting down its expenses, and learning to live within its income is the only prescription ..." Edward Bansfield, author of the widely read *The Unheavenly City*, bluntly added:

> I don't see what's to stop the unions from shaking the city down for whatever money it can accumulate. The laws have prohibited striking all along, but it's a practical problem – how do you put 30,000 or 40,000 striking teachers or policemen in jail? Obviously you don't, and if you fine them you have to put back in their pockets what you take out.

Nathan Glazer: "I think there has to be a serious confrontation with the trade unions. The fact is that we're transferring an awful lot of money to the Arabs and everybody has to chip in. We have to figure out a way of providing more services with less highly paid employees."

Lewis Mumford, author of *The City in History* and a long established urban authority, said: "Make the patient as comfortable as possible; it's too late to operate" (before adding that the government should stop spending money on "genocidal war and nuclear warfare").

For her part Jane Jacobs lamented: "New York stopped being creative a long time ago. The notion that the city could live on financial and white-collar services was nonsense...All this talk about attracting industries is nonsense. You don't attract industries to a city. Towns attract industries from cities, not cities from towns. Cities can't attract industries – they grow them."

If the 1973 CIA-backed coup against Allende in Chile and Pinochet's ensuing partnership with the Chicago School of Economics represents a decisive step toward neoliberalism, New York's example came a few short years later. Between its loss of democracy to unelected boards dominated by bankers and lawyers, the budget cuts and austerity, New York acted as an incubator for the widespread IMF imposed austerity "structural adjustment programs" in the aftermath of the debt crisis of the early 1980s that did so much to proliferate the growth of slums worldwide.[12] Decades later we can see where this all led: a world of vast wealth and staggering inequality. In that sense New York, with its large homeless population and gilded wealth, is a fitting microcosm.

Chapter 3

In what was perhaps the most memorable moment of his forgettable 2016 presidential campaign, during a debate in the Republican primaries, Ted Cruz uttered the phrase "New York values" as a smear to New Yorker Donald Trump's conservative credibility. Even before his explanation of, "I think most people know exactly what New York values are, everybody understands that the values in New York City are socially liberal, pro-abortion, or pro-gay marriage, focus around money and the media," it was probably apparent to most what Cruz meant. Trump, while not specifically targeting New York, would get into a similar act himself painting Hillary Clinton (and Cruz's wife) as tools of Goldman Sachs, and the finance industry in general, by way of her enormous speaker fees – this of course before Trump promptly appointed numerous Goldman Sachs alums to his administration. Then there was Trump's inauguration speech featuring the imagery of "American Carnage," meaning in his vernacular, cities overrun by violence and illegal immigrants.

Libertinism, violence, banks, immigrants – that covers almost every pillar of conservative populist mythology, all that is missing is the dreaded "socialism" and that has never been overly difficult to spot, especially in cities with many "foreigners" and a recent history of strong unions; New York being by far the largest city in the country and obviously the most prominent, it has long been a symbol and target for such imagery. These pillars are easy to simply mock, or at least muddy. Whatever kernel of truth there is to such sentiments, an obvious contradiction is apparent. As we've seen, despite all the police-themed TV shows, crime has stayed consistently low in New York for the past 25 years, ahead of the overall national decline, while tourism is at an all-time high. For all the elites congregating on the Upper East Side, New York has a poverty rate well above the national average.

Of course all this has an obvious political bent. Suburbanization, and its inherent mythologies of a "consumer republic" and "homeowners society" with its picket fences and shopping malls, has always been seen by its boosters, from McCarthy in the 1940s to Ted Cruz today, as both the incubator and reinforcement of a conservative status quo and a bulwark against progressive alternatives. Major American institutions from the Senate to the Electoral College feature an inherent bias against large cities. Republican presidential candidates have won three of the last seven presidential elections despite winning the popular vote only once. If current demographic trends continue, by 2030 an Electoral College majority will be possible with only 44.75 percent of the vote. On election night in 2016 the Republicans took 22 of 34 Senate seats, for a majority of 52, despite receiving 10,500,000 less overall Senate votes. When the Senate gets to work North Dakota (pop. 757,952), South Dakota (pop. 865,454), and Wyoming (pop. 585,501) have six Senators to represent their 2.2 million people while New York City's 8.5 million people, within a state of 20 million, must make due with two Senators.

If population growth is often measured as a sign of a city's success, under US law it is a means for actually weakening a city's political power. This was the clear motivation for the 2012 Republican platform's rejection of UN agenda 21 regarding sustainable development – i.e. development that makes suburbs more urban. It is the reason the Koch brothers, besides their substantial fossil fuel investments, have spent millions in opposing public transportation efforts in places like Nashville, Indianapolis, Los Angeles. Perhaps Nate Silver put the Republican perspective most succinctly when he quipped: "If a place has sidewalks, it votes Democratic."

In December 2018, in the aftermath of the previous month's midterm election, the Republican speaker of the Wisconsin

State Assembly argued that his legislative majority, despite being elected by a minority of votes, had more legitimacy than the incoming Democratic governor, who received a plurality, because, "if you took Madison and Milwaukee out of the state election formula, we would have a clear majority...We would have all five constitutional officers and we would probably have many more seats in the Legislature."

Certainly this anti-urbanism has been a strain in American thought that goes back to the founders. Thomas Jefferson famously glorified his mythical nation of independent yeoman farmers in his *Notes on the State of Virginia*. As for city dwellers Jefferson wrote:

> The mobs of great cities add just so much to the support of pure government, as sores do to the strength of the human body. It is the manners and spirit of a people which preserve a republic in vigour. A degeneracy in these is a canker which soon eats to the heart of its laws and constitution.

A century later the Populists were battling with eastern capital and investment houses over the shape of Western development. The highpoint of the Populist movement is often said to be the Omaha Platform which launched the Populist Party in 1892. While the Omaha Platform properly railed against war and trusts there was a resolution that read:

> That we condemn the fallacy of protecting American labor under the present system, which opens our ports to the pauper and criminal classes of the world and crowds out our wage-earners; and we denounce the present ineffective laws against contract labor, and demand the further restriction of undesirable emigration.

The sentiment in play here is producerism. This is simply

defined as a conviction that the wealth produced in a society should belong to its producers. If obvious nobility can be found in such a sentiment the problem is its targets run both ways. Producerism doesn't quite spare the rich and rent seeking, but its main target has always been an allegedly parasitic poor. In the United States the parasites have always been easy to label: immigrants, blacks, other minorities. This sort of producerism is perfect for an anti-urban view as both the blood-sucking bankers and dirty hordes can be placed in the same cities.

Sometime in the fall of 1972, a few years before Ford's infamous "Drop Dead" speech to New York, Richard Nixon was taped in an unhinged rant that included the words "Goddamn New York," then adding that it is a place filled with "Jews and Catholics and blacks and Puerto Ricans." Then in conclusion stating there is a "law of the jungle where some things don't survive...Maybe New York shouldn't survive. Maybe it should go through a cycle of destruction."

The Cold War saw anti-urbanism translated into national defense. Figuring that dense urban populations presented a more inviting nuclear missile target for Russian aggression, in 1951 the *Bulletin of Atomic Scientists* titled an issue "Defense Through Decentralization" advocating that large urban cores be dispersed into smaller settlements – in the event of nuclear war the less population density per square mile apparently means less death per missile strike. A year earlier *Collier's* published a cover story: "Hiroshima, USA: Can Anything be Done About It?" The lead illustration featured a mushroom cloud over Manhattan.

Destruction, in cinematic and literary form, is something New York has gone through countless times. In his epic *Ecology of Fear*, Mike Davis remarked regarding Los Angeles: "No city, in fiction, or film, has been more likely to figure as the icon of a really bad future (or present, for that matter)." He could have added "except New York." Choose a time period, find its apocalyptic threat, and the destruction of New York by said threat is a given.

Back in 1881 Park Benjamin Jr's *The End of New York* had the city meet its fate at the hands of the ironclad ships of the Spanish Navy. Benjamin was apparently concerned about American navel defenses, the book an attempt to drum up support for increased military spending. This a mere 17 years before the US delivered the coup de grace to the decrepit Spanish Empire in 1898. In 1890 Ignatius Donnelly published his bestselling *Ceasar's Column: A Story of the Twentieth Century*. Donnelly, who would go on to write the platform for the Populist Party, had New York's destruction the result of a proletarian uprising by the Brotherhood of Destruction against the ruling oligarchy (the action takes place a century forward in 1988). Ceasar's Column refers to a mass grave emanating from Union Square seen by the main character, Gabriel Weltsein, fleeing the city in an airship. In 1907 the great HG Wells, in *The War in the Air,* gave New York over to German air bombardment ironically foreshadowing the fate of German cities at the hands of the allies during World War II.

Hollywood of course has this destruction feature down to assembly line efficiency. New York has seen its end due to aliens (*Independence Day*, along with other much resented cities LA and DC), every kind of climatic/ecological event (*The Day After Tomorrow, Category 7, Volcano in New York*), asteroids, and turned into a maximum-security prison (*Escape From New York*).

In *The City's End: Two Centuries of Fantasies, Fear, and Premonitions of New York's Destruction*, Max Page writes:

> We destroy New York on film and paper to bound the fear of natural and manmade disaster…to escape the sense of inevitable and incomprehensible economic transformations, by telling stories of clear and present dangers, with causes and effect, villians and heros, to make our world comprehensible than it has become.[1]

If there is one thing Hollywood can be said to have mastered it is cheap escapism. And obviously skyscrapers and other iconic urban markers make greater spectacle for disaster porn than sprawl. Still it is not difficult to see the Freudian aspect to it all. Obviously all this is a two-way street. While cities have been victims of anti-urban ideologies, cities have a long history of boosterism that has ranged from the brilliant to the bizarre. In what was perhaps his swan-song to New York, Robert Moses organized the World's Fair which took place in two 6-month sessions from April 1964 to October 1965. The Disney designed fair was marketed as a festival for "Peace Through Understanding" and dedicated to "Man's achievement on a Shrinking Globe in an Expanding Universe" (it was at the World's Fair that Disney unveiled its "It's a Small World" ride and song at a UNICEF pavilion sponsored by Pepsi). Constructed by Coca Cola, RCA, Ford, and Disney, Moses strictly prohibited a "Coney Island atmosphere"; it was a bland spread of corporate logos and high art.

By the end the Fair fell short of Moses' projection of visitors by 20 million. While it generated $750 million in spending, Moses had predicted $5-8 billion. The Fair Corporation would lose $200 million to investors – New York's taxpayers would end up $50 million in the red just as budget deficits were beginning to add up. The World's Fair lasting legacy to New York is a tasteless metal globe in Flushing-Meadows Park.

In his excellent *Branding New York: How a City in Crisis Was Sold to The World*, Miriam Greenberg explains the aftermath of this for New York's corporate boosters in the increasingly anti-urban context of the 1960s:

> Under such conditions, it became clear that old-fashioned urban boosters was essentially powerless – even it echoed the grandeur of the New York World's Fair. Indeed, the Fair may be seen as the last hurrah of New York's booster tradition and

a transitional moment in the city's approach to marketing itself to the world.[2]

The process can backfire in other ways. A few years later Mayor John Lindsay was labeling New York "fun city" (that he first called New York a fun city in the middle of the 1966 transit strike invited some ridicule). Lindsay is generally regarded as a failed mayor, the one most responsible for the crisis that exploded in the mid-1970s, but with his promotion of the arts he did leave a lasting legacy on the city. His rezoning of the theater district to allow taller buildings if owners kept theaters in the bottom floors helped reverse a decline in shows and led to an expansion of four new theaters by 1974. Broadway was one of the few bright economic spots during the crisis. It remains a vital part of the city's cultural fabric.

Of greater consequence for New York's image, the Lindsay administration streamlined the process of filming movies in the city, creating a new Office of Television, Broadcasting, and Film to greatly reduce the amount of paperwork needed to film. For all its national prominence, in 1965 only 13 feature films were shot in New York due to a labyrinth of bureaucracy. Lindsay's initiative had the desired effect: an average of 46 movies a year were filmed in the city during his two terms as mayor and the film industry has become a large source of jobs in the present[3]. Unfortunately for New York's reputation many of the most famous of those films made during the Lindsay years and soon after portrayed the city as a dark, chaotic, urban thunderdome. *Sleeper, The French Connection, Panic in Needle Park, Mean Streets, Taxi Driver, Serpico, The Taking of Pelham One Two Three, Fort Apache, the Bronx*; if it was the golden age of Hollywood directorship it left New York's reputation stained to this day. Even today during an age of low crime TV and movies, theaters are still jammed with New York based crime stories.

Then there is boosterism of another kind. In June 1975 leaflets emblazoned with a hooded gothic skull were drawn up titled *Fear City: A Survival Guide for Visitors to the City of New York*. The leaflet featured the statement that: "The best advice we can give you is this: until things change, stay away from New York City if you possibly can." If a trip was absolutely necessary tourists should stay off the street after 6pm. If you must leave your hotel summon a taxi, stay in Manhattan, and avoid the subways. The uproar generated coverage as far away as the *Chicago Tribune* and *San Francisco Chronicle*, particularly considering the source of the leaflet was the CPS made up of city unions including the 24 police and fire unions. The purpose was to pressure the Beame administration into rescinding almost 11,000 planned layoffs of uniformed officers.

After a flurry of court battles and media bombast, where the first amendment rights of the CPS came out ahead, the Fear City campaign was suspended in the face of public outrage. Very few leaflets ended up being passed out. The proposed budget cuts went through though they were predictably targeted to working-class neighborhoods in the "outer" boroughs.

This was also the time of deindustrialization and corporate exodus. New York lost an average of 100,000 jobs a year from 1970-74. Deindustrialization began earlier, the effects of which were tamed somewhat by the huge expansion of office jobs in the late 1960s. By the early 1970s a corporate exodus was underway. Older northeastern cities saw their factories and corporations decamping to the suburbs and sunbelt. New York lost 30 percent of its share of Fortune 500 companies between 1968 and 1974.[4] Johnny Carson's escape from New York to Hollywood symbolized the decline of New York's overall image. The powers that be felt the need for a new and thorough approach.

The main impetus for the CPS to call off the Fear City campaign was its negotiations with a group called the Association for a Better New York (ABNY). The association proclaims on its current webpage:

ABNY is a non-profit organization dedicated to the constant growth and renewal of New York City's people, businesses and communities. We are a coalition of business, labor, non-profit and political leaders focused on exploring and implementing ideas that keep the city moving forward.

ABNY was founded in 1971 by Lew Rudin, then the CEO of Rudin Management, a powerful real estate empire, in partnership with Alton Marshall, who served as chief of staff for Governor Rockefeller before taking over the Rockefeller Group and Rockefeller Center, Inc. Its purpose was to organize real estate and corporate interests in a coherent agenda for the city and to position itself to be able to implement that agenda. This would include research, marketing, and lobbying in a public-private partnership.

The origins of the nickname "The Big Apple" aren't clear. Despite New York State being one of the largest producers of apples in the country, the name appears unrelated to apple growing. The main theory is that around 1920 a New York reporter named John Fitz Gerald overheard a group of stable hands in New Orleans say they were going racing in "The Big Apple" – New York's race tracks being considered the most prestigious (a similar variation has a jockey telling his horse if he won in New York he'd win "the big Apple"). From there the phrase moved to jazz musicians. By the 1930s New York had clearly surpassed Chicago (which had previously surpassed New Orleans) as the epicenter for jazz – "The Big Apple."

Whatever its origins the name was revived by the ABNY campaign of the early 1970s. Through the "Apple Polishing Corp" ABNY organized an army of employees all over Midtown to sweep sidewalks in front of their workplaces every morning. It also produced thousands of golden apple pins and stickers and handed them out in business centers from City Hall to The Four Seasons.

Other ABNY initiatives were related to crime. It paid for bullet proof vests for the entire NYPD, purchased a radio frequency from the Federal Communications Commission (FCC) and a transmitter, and passed out walkie-talkies to thousands of doormen, as well as financing the first 24-hour closed circuit TV cameras for Times Square.

Of greater significance the ABNY website takes credit for spearheading the "I Love New York" campaign (this can be debated). The campaign itself is the stuff of legend. Aimed at boosting tourism, the campaign was the state and city's first international, yearlong marketing campaign. Its origins go back to a luncheon in the headquarters of Union Carbide. The company was fleeing New York, apparently due to the inability to get tourists to visit. This led the new deputy commissioner for the New York State Department of Commerce (DOC), John Doyle, to an awakening. Doyle halted all tourism spending as it was and put the money into New York State's first professional market research.

The result was the "I Love New York." The TV and print campaign was designed by the firm Wells, Rich, Greene (WRG) and featured the omnipresent logo designed by Milton Glaser. The campaign would create its own jingle about the attractions of trips to New York, fortunately that doggerel didn't have long-term staying power but in 1977 it was sung from the Broadway stage. Broadway in 1977 did feature the first runs for *Annie* and *A Chorus Line* along with *Greece* and *The King and I* adding pizzazz to the television spots. Studio 54 even unveiled a disco version and for the night of the celebration of the campaign's launch, buildings throughout the city lit up to spell out the logo. That logo can still easily be found today.

It is a fact that tourism greatly increased in the late 1970s. It went up over 300 percent. However, the direct impact of the I Love New York campaign was never established. An audit by the State Controller found that "without considering other factors that affect vacation habits," the DOC wasn't capable of establishing a "causal relationship" between the campaign and increased tourism.

Whatever the practical results, the campaign did signify a new beginning. Symbolizing this was the increased spending on attracting tourists in the aftermath of New York's fiscal crisis at the same time that the city's total budget was being cut. From then on it would be urban planning based on branding, tourism, and finance. And at least at first it would be Manhattan based. Back to Miriam Greenberg:

> I Love New York was a crowning achievement in the effort to "purge" the city of its liberal ways in the wake of the fiscal crisis, but did little to address the growing needs of the city's population. Rather, the campaign ushered in a new model of economic recovery that emphasized short-term strategies like city branding and incentives for business over and above long-term investments in public infrastructure, collective consumption, and the support of a mixed economic base.[5]

As we've seen, beginning with Nixon and continuing through Reagan and beyond, the federal government began withdrawing funding from cities. American cities, beginning with New York, responded by adopting a neoliberal strategy, subsidizing businesses, and attracting high-income residents and tourists. One idea was taxes on high earners would make up for what used to be funded by federal spending. This was no hidden policy whispered in dark corners of City Hall. Mayor Koch would be quoted as saying: "We're not catering to the poor anymore. There are four other boroughs for them to live in. They don't have to live in Manhattan."[6] This was not an appeal to libertarian tough love. By no means did the subsidizing cease. In this light it only shifted recipients, and in ways that are too often discounted.

There was the J-51 tax abatement. Originally established by

the city in 1955 for bringing hot water to flats, it gave landlords a 12-year exemption from increases in property assessments and a 20-year abatement of their property taxes up to 90 percent of the costs of a major rehabilitation. In the midst of economic crisis in the 1970s the abatement was expanded to include commercial space and hotels. In 1977 the program cost the city around $11 million a year. By 1984, toward the end of Koch's second term, the cost was up to $117 million[7]. As developers in downtown and Midtown were given most of the largesse, the buildings most affected were Single Room Occupancy (SRO) hotels that housed the poor. An estimated 100,000 SRO units were lost during the 1970s and 80s, converted to higher rent housing or hotels.

The infamous 421-a program, limited in the 1980s to central Manhattan, went from costing the city $70 million in 1984 to $197 million by 1991[8]. There were the individually negotiated tax reductions that cost the city hundreds of millions of dollars between 1977 and 1981 (estimates range from $233 to $600 million). These were meant to coax businesses from leaving the city, a standard tactic for businesses to strong arm cities though it's often dubious when it comes to flagships leaving Manhattan, especially as the city's real estate market had rebounded by that point.

In 1982 the city put forward the Midtown Development Plan. The purpose here was to stimulate office space on the Westside where historically there hadn't been much, or much need. The official justification was the East Side was getting overcrowded, though powerful interests were behind policies for increasing property values on the West Side – the Rockefellers would conveniently sell Rockefeller Center to the Mitsubishi Estate Company in 1989.The city would add 53 million square feet of office space, a 22 percent increase, during the 1980s[9] (mirroring the subsidized boom in office buildings of the late 1960s that foreshadowed the crash of the mid-1970s). The subsidized boom of the 1980s would foreshadow Black Monday in October 1987.

That construction was being initiated months afterward shows the boom was largely subsidy driven rather than market driven. All told developmental subsidies would cost the city a billion a year by 1988.[10]

To get a sense of the spiraling of the process, fast forward 3 decades from Koch's policies and see that billionaire mayor Michael Bloomberg was quoted regarding other billionaires: "They are the ones that pay a lot of taxes. They're the ones that spend a lot of money in the stores and restaurants and create a big chunk of our economy...If we could get every billionaire around the world to move here, it would be a godsend."

This shift was reflected perfectly in film and literature. Crime-based themes by no means disappeared from New York based movies, and such themes played a large part in Tom Wolfe's novel *Bonfire of the Vanities* and Oliver Stone's *Wall Street*, probably the most timeless works from the period, but the mid-to-late 80s saw the likes of *Bright Lights Big City*, *The Secret of My Success*, *Working Girl*, *Desperately Seeking Susan*, among others that portrayed the city as a world of ambition and financial decadence rather than only a concrete jungle.

Another key component was policing. Contrary to popular belief it was the Dinkins administration that brought the legendary squeegee men to heel. It is telling that this minor annoyance became the symbol of what is considered the dawn of a new era of policing. Even in the present day, New York's ostensibly progressive mayor Bill de Blasio has consistently defended broken windows policing even as he has backed off some of its harshness (to the disappointment of many, the city's crime numbers have remained low). The point is that broken windows both preceded and outlived Rudy Giuliani's election and his hiring of Bill Bratton as police commissioner (Bratton would be brought back to the job by de Blasio).

What is telling about the squeegee men is that they committed very few crimes, and any crimes were incidental to what they were actually known for which was simply attempting to clean windshields for money at busy traffic points. The image of the squeegee men didn't summon visions of violence. Rather it was an idea of disorder. The roots of it go back to the mid-1980s. Just as city planning was converting low-income housing to high-end housing and accelerating deindustrialization, with property values rising as a result of zoning and city subsidies (precisely the point) New York lost nearly 25 percent of its manufacturing jobs from the beginning of the 1980s to Black Monday, meanwhile the crack epidemic was gaining steam. The Go-Go 80s with an exploding finance industry polarized inequality, and higher property values pushed developers to build for the high end of the market. Homelessness and panhandling predictably became hot issues.

Inevitably in such a context even more liberal neighborhoods come to support policies that can be described as draconian. Grand Central Station became an early flashpoint. Grand Central had become an obvious gathering spot for the homeless. This had a detrimental effect on surrounding real estate values spurring local businesses to form a Business Improvement District (BID). BIDs were legalized in state law in 1981. A BID is basically a group of local businesses that pool money to take over, or at least supplement, the cleaning and security of their local area. New York now has about 75 such groups, raising serious questions about democratic control. To whom after all are they accountable? Where do non-property holders stand? What values, if any, do these local business groups enforce? Given that an extra tax is required, BID would seem to inherently favor wealthier property owners who have a greater motivation to push out cheaper commercial tenants. BIDs' organizational structure often gives greater voting power to those within the BID with the most valuable property, further exacerbating that trend. In 1989 the Grand Central Partnership (GCP) created a uniformed security force, along with the Metro North and

Metropolitan Transit Authority (MTA), that banned washing clothes in the restroom, giving away food, occupying more than one seat, and creating excessive noise. While these reforms didn't initially have much success the GCP was able to lobby the NYPD, by essentially threatening its authority, to a more draconian approach. The Grand Central BID would eventually be disbanded by the city for issuing bonds without the city's permission.[11]

BIDs have also at times been a source of extremely exploitive labor. In 2000 GCP and the 34th Street Partnership BIDs settled, after 7 years, a lawsuit charging that they paid employees as little as $1 an hour to walk security patrols and clean toilets. The obvious reason the BIDs dragged the lawsuits on was in the hope that the workers, often homeless people, would fade away. It was Sonia Sotomayor, then a federal district court judge, who found the BIDs, run by well paid executives, guilty of breaking minimum wage laws.[12]

When Giuliani became mayor and appointed Bratton, previously commissioner of Transit Police (the Transit Police would merge with the NYPD in 1995) Broken Windows became a sensation. At bottom broken windows is an extremely conservative philosophy that posits aggressive policing as the main answer to all social ills (i.e. disorder) thereby downplaying, in fact often acting in concert with, policies that exacerbate social and economic inequality, shifting the blame for that inequality on to the victims themselves. In New York this fell under the banner of "quality of life," the targets during the Giuliani years included at different points the homeless, street vendors, happy hours, and jay walkers – the latter Giuliani increased the fine for from two dollars up to 50 dollars (fortunately cops basically refused to enforce it).

Along with high-profile innovation was Compstat. Whatever the insights of statistical analysis in any field, an endemic drawback is that it provokes a dependence on numbers and quantity over quality. Local precincts were given quotas for summonses. That was always officially denied by the NYPD, despite evidence; however, the NYPD does acknowledge "performance goals." Needless to say the brunt of the numbers approach fell heavily on poorer minority neighborhoods. According to the ACLU 81 percent of the 7.3 million people summonsed from 2001 to 2013 were Black and Hispanic. A *New York Daily News* analysis in September 2014 showed just how stark the discrepancies are: For summons that listed race data (those that listed the race of the person receiving the summons), based on data from the Office of Court Administration on 6.9 million criminal summons issued from 2001-13, blacks and Hispanics received an absurd 91 percent of the summons issued for failure to have a dog license (the Department of Health estimates that less than 17 percent of dogs citywide are licensed), 92 percent for spitting, 83 percent for consumption of alcohol on streets, and 84 percent for Bicycle on Sidewalk (riding), among many others.[13] The same holds true for marijuana arrests. While marijuana arrests have been down since de Blasio took office, arrests for marijuana have long been focused on blacks and Hispanics. The *New York Times* found that in the three previous years black people are arrested eight times the rate of whites (in Manhattan the rate of black arrest is 15 times higher), Hispanics five times the rate. The NYPD's initial stated justification was that more complaint calls for marijuana came from Black and Hispanic neighborhoods. However, the *Times* cited police data that shows neighborhoods with similar numbers of calls to 911 or 311 still showed large racial disparities. In Queens predominantly black Queens Village had an arrest rate ten times as high as Forest Hills which has a small black population. In Brooklyn the largely black neighborhood of Canarsie had a rate four times as high as whiter Greenpoint.[14]

Again this policy of reaction would spiral upward to the Bloomberg administration's infamous stop-and-frisk policy.

According to the NYPD's Annual Reports (available on the ACLU's webpage[15]) there were 97,296 stops by police in 2002. In 2003 it was up to 160,851 stops. By 2006 that number reached 506,491; with the exception of 2007 (472,096) the number of stops would exceed half a million every year reaching the surreal 685,724 stops in 2011. The number of stops would decline from there until a federal judge ruled the practice unconstitutional. The de Blasio administration dropped the city's appeal upon taking office. The number of stops has consistently declined since, in 2017 stops declined to 10,861.

It would be disingenuous to argue that stop-and-frisk put a serious dent in crime. The city's murder rate made by far its biggest drop before Bloomberg was in office. The Giuliani years, for all their high-profile incidents of police violence, didn't feature nearly as high numbers of stop-and-frisks which went up more than 600 percent under Bloomberg. In 2002, Bloomberg's first year as mayor, there were 1892 shooting victims. The year 2011, with the astronomical number of stops, still saw 1821 shooting victims. In close to 90 percent of stops during Bloomberg's three terms those stopped were totally innocent and about the same number were Black or Hispanic. The most touted justification for the policy was stopping violent crime: guns were found in less than 0.2 percent of stops (overall murders went down 19 percent from 2001-11).

Though stop-and-frisk has greatly declined under the de Blasio administration, there are still trends toward expanding policing. The administration funded 1000 more officers, including the creation of a special anti-terrorist "Strategic Response Group" that, before backtracking, Bratton declared would be used to deal with events like the city's "recent protests" (presumably this referred to the protests against alleged police brutality in the aftermath of Eric Gardner's death). Meanwhile the NYPD's gang database has expanded by 70 percent since 2014. On average that is 342 names a month added to the database, three times the rate of the previous decade. According to NYPD numbers 66 percent of names added from December 2013 to February 2018 were black, 33 percent were Hispanic. Gang motivated crime accounts for less than 1 percent of reported crime in the city.[16]

A result of the shift in policing and development was the transforming of the commercial landscape. Evidence suggests that neighborhoods facing gentrification pressures saw an increase in 311 and 911 calls. As demographics shift social norms and expectations shift, "quality of life" issues around noise, loitering come to the foreground (paradoxically where there's gentrification, there's always an influx of bars). Such would easily describe New York in the 1990s and 2000s. If broken windows policing was oppressive to its many nonviolent victims it had the effect of clearing the way for bigger business.

Not that there aren't more overt police actions around the same theme. In one high-profile incident in Harlem on October 17, 1994 Giuliani sent hundreds of cops dressed in riot gear to clear street vendors on 125th St. While conflict between the street vendors and stores was somewhat endemic, and undoubtedly before the sweep the street could be cluttered, riot police were never previously employed on this level (an earlier attempted crackdown 2 years earlier was called off). The sweep was supported by the 125th Street BID and some local politicians. In the aftermath, much as in the rest of the city, even as crime declined arrests for low level drug crimes increased.

The year 1994 also saw the Clinton Administration sign federal legislation creating the Upper Manhattan Empowerment Zone (UMEZ), a federal grant of $100 million plus $250 million in tax credits. Much of this was focused on outside capital rather than empowering local business, mainly in the form of using public sector funding to leverage private sector loans.[17] An early project was Harlem USA, a 275,000 square foot shopping center anchored by the Magic Johnson multiplex theater (Disney was a tenant for a few years). From there the chain stores moved in and property values shot up displacing many longtime smaller businesses. Establishments such as Bobby's Happy House, the first black-owned business on the street, opened in 1946, and Copeland's restaurant, among others, once gave 125th Street its flavor but fell to the new environment. The famous M&G Diner, renowned for its southern food, closed in 2008 as did the Boro Hotel. The Lenox Lounge, a bar that once featured performances by Miles Davis and John Coltrane, closed in 2012 after its rent doubled. By 2006 the number of chain stores in Central Harlem had tripled. After a Bloomberg rezoning in 2008, 125th Street featured Banana Republic, DSM, the Gap, and dozens more such chain stores and banks. As if announcing a sort of finality, Whole Foods opened in 2017.

For decades another center for African-American commercial and cultural life has been Downtown Brooklyn. In the aftermath of the 2004 rezoning, one BID pushing here was the Fulton Mall Improvement Association, the board of which is a real estate and political who's who. The Albee Square Mall, the locally legendary shopping and cultural spot that served as a platform for small black-owned businesses (immortalized by rapper Biz Markie's 1988 song "Albee Square Mall"), was bulldozed. One estimate is that over 100 small businesses, many of which served the local Caribbean population, have closed since to be replaced by the usual banalities such as Raymond & Flanigan, Shake Shack, GAP Century 21, H & M, and Armani among others.

Fulton Street is the third busiest shopping area in the city. Visit Herald Square, one that is busier, and one will find largely the same selection, certainly the identical overall tone. Union Square has long been a site for protest and art. Even visiting today one has a decent chance to catch a group drawing attention to a noble cause, though in a more restricted setting thanks to Union Square's BID. Yet such protest groups are surrounded by corporate dominance. Of the roughly four dozen stores surrounding the park virtually none are independent, and all can be found elsewhere. The BID for Union Square is the Union Square Partnership. It hasn't been shy in its sentiment. A spokesman was once quoted as saying: "We're constantly trying to attract a specific demographic: young, moneyed, consumers who know New York City from *New York Magazine*...and who watch Friends." Further uptown on Columbus Circle sits Time Warner Center, a "vertical" mall opened in 2003. There Whole Foods, H&M, Sephora, and J-Crew could be found. Amazon has its first New York "brick and mortar" bookstore. In Williamsburg the 2005 rezoning increased commercial gentrification that outpaced even demographic change. Research shows that in a 20-block area of central Williamsburg, 90 percent of the more than 50 bars and restaurants are less than a decade old replacing Hispanic-owned businesses that long served the neighborhood's largely Hispanic population. The number of Hispanic-owned businesses dropped by half in the years immediately following the rezoning, far outpacing changes in the local population at the time.[18] Following a 2009 rezoning of Coney Island, with the assistance of Hurricane Sandy in 2013, disaster capitalism often being the efficient form, chains have moved in hard on Surf Avenue while Coney Island's world famous amusement parks have been shrunk and its historical buildings demolished. During Bloomberg's second term the number of small business loans dropped an astronomical 500 percent while the number of commercial eviction warrants numbered nearly 29,000. True this period overlapped with the great recession; however, the largest turnover took place in gentrifying neighborhoods where commercial rents were rising.

Further downtown, in fact throughout the city, storefronts sit empty as landlords hold out for higher rent paying chains or multinational bank branches. In fact a 2018 survey by Morgan Stanley and Douglas Elliman determined that an incredible 20 percent of Manhattan's street retail is vacant or soon to become vacant. Over the past 3 years the number of retail workers has fallen by more than 10,000 each year. Many would point to the dominance of Amazon, and the general expansion of ecommerce, as the primary reason for New York's expanding retail desert. Whatever the effect of online shopping, no doubt a factor, there's an obvious reason to suspect it's not the biggest factor. From 2010 to 2014 commercial rents in Manhattan's most trafficked shopping areas went up 89 percent according to the real estate and investment firm CBRE Group.[19] With much of New York's prime real estate in the hands of private equity, global capital, and hedge funds, such landlords have ample reserves to warehouse property and wait for the highest rents.

Of course nothing signifies New York's commercial transformation like Times Square. While Giuliani boosters, not to mention Giuliani himself, like to take Times Square's redevelopment as another feather in his cap, the roots of the redevelopment go back to the Koch years. Legislation requiring a certain, high amount of light to emanate from buildings was passed by the Board of Estimate in 1987. It was during the 1980s that the 42nd Street Development Project was created by city and state officials. This project established a 13-acre renewal site for two city blocks between Broadway and 8th Avenue. The parameters for the redevelopment were in place (established by the design firm Cooper and Eckstut).

The presence of Disney is taken to be the flagship and symbol of the redevelopment. The heavily subsidized deal that brought Disney to Times Square was started with the Dinkins administration. As should be apparent by now, the beauty of gaining one prominent corporate brand means that others should be following on its heels. Disney went one better, insisting that two nationally recognized entertainment brands had to sign agreements to open on the same block. Disney signed on to restore the New Amsterdam Theater, the longstanding Lion King show started there in 1997. Madame Tussaud's wax museum would appear up the street in 2000. The redevelopment, mainly in the form of new office towers, was completed under Giuliani's watch, thanks largely to the end of the recession of the early 1990s. Giuliani's big contribution, another Disney request, was the infamous zoning legislation outlawing adult establishments within 500 feet of residential areas, places of worship, schools, and other adult establishments. In June 2017 the Court of Appeals upheld a 2001 city law that expanded what can be considered "adult" entertainment to stores that even offer explicit imagery[20].

The old Times Square didn't exactly go down without a fight, landlords prospering off the sex industry fought the redevelopment for years. Though it became raunchier and male dominated as time went by the sex industry in Times Square preceded even the subways. While popular images bring to mind creeps and perverts, porn brought in big money. A study by sociologists at City University of New York, cited by Lynne Sagalyn in her *Times Square Roulette*, estimated that the average peep show brought in a weekly gross from $74,000 to $106,000, about $5 million a year.[21]

This was just before the Internet was to revolutionize the porn industry, perhaps making traditional porn shops somewhat obsolete (though it's worth pointing out that in November 2017 a seasonal shop opened by Pornhub, consisting mostly of sex toys and Pornhub sweatshirts, drew quite a large opening day line). Simply lamenting the decline of Times Square porn is hardly the point. Porn remains omnipresent in the world. Concepts like authenticity, and organic, can be dangerous words, as well as meaningless ones. However, perhaps like Supreme Court Justice Potter Stewart's defining of pornography back in 1964 as, "I know it when I see it," some level of authenticity and locality is obvious. One wonders if the throngs of tourists that daily clog Times Square traveled their many miles to see another Disney Store or to pose at Madame Tussaud's then dine at Applebee's or Bubba Gump Shrimp. Or do all the flashing TVs simply do the trick?

The "development," the broken windows policing, the triumph of order, the endlessly monotonous shopping, the countless chain pharmacies, it all amounted to the suburbization of the city. It goes back to the time capital abandoned cities like New York for the suburbs. The response of the city was to become suburban. The grand irony of the lingering anti-New York sentiment coming from the heartland is that New York has spent the last 4 decades dulling most of its urban edge – i.e. becoming in a sense more conservative.

Jonny Aspen, of the Oslo School of Architecture and Design, coined the term "zombie urbanism," which he describes as "the effect to create a city environment that is perceived as attractive to the well-being and cultural-interested middle class." In an interview with Jerimiah Moss' blog Vanishing New York, Aspen elaborated: "What we can see is a kind of staged urbanism in which there is no room for irregularity and the unexpected, a well-designed, neat, and tedious urbanism based on a simplified understanding of the urban combined with more ideal aspirations about creating 'living' and 'people friendly' cities."'[22]

In addition to physical space there is the increasing effect of digital space. Platforms like Airbnb and Foursquare are, as Igor Schwarzmann, co-founder of Third Wave explains, producing a "harmonization of tastes." Get off a plane or bus in any prominent American city and more than likely one will encounter the same landscape as in the last city. Chain stores are just one prominent layer. How many factories converted into restaurants or clubs while keeping the industrial sheen, local coffee shops in industrial chic? If SoHo in Lower Manhattan with its converted lofts was an original trendy post-industrial neighborhood, it has spawned SoMa in San Francisco, SoWa in Boston, and NoMa in Washington DC.

The history of a place is marketed by both city planners and developers as real estate with the express purpose of wiping that very history away. The rezoning plan for Downtown Brooklyn mixed praise for the Fulton Street commercial scene with the idea that stores that would be displaced "do not have substantial economic value to the City, they do not define neighborhood character, nor do they belong to a special category of business that is protected by special regulations or publicly adopted plans." Christopher Mele puts it insightfully, in a way that can be applied to neighborhoods from Harlem to Bed Stuy, in *Selling the Lower East Side: Culture, Real Estate, and Resistance in New York City*

> In the East Village, real estate developers have translated the symbolic value of cultural difference into economic value, attracting middle-class renters, diners, and shoppers who find allure in this edgier version of "bohemian mix," flush with modern living spaces and other amenities…The architectural features and interior designs of the East Village's new, high-end commercial and residential spaces produce a contrived sense of urban grittiness and feel of "downtown" without the risks and inconveniences of poverty.[23]

Today the branding machine is churning like never before. Upon assuming office in 2002 Bloomberg immediately started talking about New York's brand. In keeping with the neoliberal competition between cities, in his first State of the City, he mused:

> New York is in a fierce, worldwide competition. We must offer the best product and sell it forcefully…We'll take advantage of our brand. New York is the best-known city on the planet… Yet as a city, we've never taken direct, coordinated custody of our image. By changing that, we can realize additional city revenues immediately.

Bloomberg went on to institute New York City Marketing, which a few years later in 2006 was merged, along with another Bloomberg created office, NYC Big Events, with NYC & Company which is "the official destination marketing organization for the five boroughs of New York City." NYC & Company's mission "is to maximize travel and tourism opportunities throughout the five boroughs, build economic prosperity and spread the dynamic image of New York City around the world." NYC & Company hired the firm Wolff Olins to design a new "NYC" logo that has become so ubiquitous it probably goes unrecognized. In 2006 Bloomberg doubled NYC & Company's city funding to $22.5 million. The operation was restructured along the lines of a professional marketing firm including a Media Department to oversee a constantly updated webpage, an Advertising Department to sell ad space, and an Entertainment Department to generate product placement – the logo and other images in movies and TV shows. NYC & Company has opened offices in and about 20 other countries.

The first official city branding campaign was the "This is New York" campaign in 2006. This was a first in that it promoted the entire city, not just Manhattan, as a family-friendly destination. Ads ran in many other countries and American cities, and of course in New York itself. If promoting the city as a whole for tourists was unthinkable in prior times, it became natural by Bloomberg's second term. Since 2006 the number of hotels has tripled in Brooklyn and doubled in Queens[24]. After that promotions were unceasing: "New York: The Real Deal" offered low budget packages for family trips; other promotions featured as family ambassadors characters from Sesame Street, to The Smurfs, to Dora the Explorer. Even the experts at times completely miss. In October 2014, on the heels of her song "Welcome to New York," easily the worst New York themed song ever, Pennsylvania born Taylor Swift was named New York's Welcome Ambassador, though native New Yorkers Jay-Z and

Alicia Keys' better but vastly overplayed anthem "Empire State of Mind" has also become a staple. The machine continues to grind under de Blasio. The latest campaign by NYC & Company is called "True York City." The $15 million campaign, extending to 16 other countries, will feature ads and billboards with the phrase "Famous Original New York City." New York & Company CEO Fred Dixon was quoted as saying: "We're encouraging travelers to New York City to go beyond the selfie, to go beyond their bucket list, and explore and engage more deeply with the destination," including visiting neighborhood shops to support local businesses. This as the NFL Experience and the Grand Old Opry open in Times Square. Estimates from NYC & Company are that New York will receive 67 million tourists in 2019, marking the tenth consecutive year of rising numbers.[25]

Like with the original "I Love New York" campaign, the exact extent of the effects of all this will never be known for sure but like many places in the world New York continues to draw record numbers of tourists every year. One problem with a tourist economy is a simple matter of space. When New York State's legislature passed a bill in October 2016 making it illegal to rent a housing unit for fewer than 30 days (or even to advertise such a listing), 20,000 such listings were on Airbnb. Hawaii, another heavily branded place that has been flooded by new record numbers of tourists every year, saw its population decline in 2017 despite low unemployment numbers. Hawaii also has one of the worst rates of homelessness in the country[26]. Locals in Venice (Italy) and Barcelona have staged protests against mass tourism, and the impact that "home sharing" platforms have on housing markets already in crisis.

As for the branding machine, whether aimed at attracting corporations or tourists, there is an obvious contradiction between a system funded with public money in the service of private interests, such as developers, hotel chains, credit card companies, etc. New York's history shows that branding campaigns accelerate during times of crisis, whether in the late 1970s, post 9/11, or in the midst of the financial crisis in 2007-08. By design, branding during such times is laced with utopian sentiment. What images of safety, family-fun, and even "diversity" convey is a consensus that transcends, or negates, politics much as Bloomberg's manufactured image as a nonpartisan, technocratic "CEO Mayor" above the political fray sought to mask the extension of corporate power in the city.

Of course all of this has not gone without resistance and as time has marched on the counterforces have achieved positive developments. Though to the extent it still exists its effects remain in minorities, thanks to the hard work of activists "stop-and-frisk" has largely been ended and discredited in New York. Crime numbers released in January 2017 revealed crime to be at the lowest since the city has been keeping reliable records. After initial reluctance de Blasio (prodded by the earlier support by Governor Cuomo and then City Council Speaker Melissa Mark-Viverito) announced an intention to close the notorious hellhole Rikers Island. A large part of that plan is cutting the prison's population in half in order to open smaller, spread out prisons. Small scale marijuana possession (less than 0.9 ounce) is no longer subject to arrest. Full legalization on the state level is gaining momentum.

Yet there is still a need for much greater reforms. Even if its edge has been dulled, "broken windows" as a philosophy is still defended. Far too many issues from homelessness, to drugs, mental illness, and prostitution are still seen through the prism of policing (this does nobody, including cops, any favors). Minorities continue to receive the bulk of summons for actions that are petty and universal.

In November 2017 the city council passed a bill reforming the commercial rent tax, which affects businesses in Manhattan south of 96th Street. When the reform came into effect in July 2018 the threshold for paying the tax increased to businesses paying $500,000 a year in rent with an annual income of $5 million, rather than the previous threshold of $250,000. Before this, the last time the tax was changed was in 2001 when it was raised to $250,000 from $150,000 a year in rent. To put it mildly commercial rents have been skyrocketing. According to the Real Estate Board of New York, from 2001-16 the rents in SoHo increased by 431 percent leading to the many empty storefronts as property owners hold out for more profitable chain stores.[27]

The Council Speaker Mark-Viverito was quoted: "You don't want every neighborhood, every block to just be pharmacies and banks. You want there to be opportunities to be smaller retailers that are locally owned, that have a history in the community. Being able to provide some relief for them is something we have to take seriously as a city."

As for pharmacies New York has more than its share with over 300 Duane Reades, along with 624 Dunkin Donuts, 207 McDonalds, 330 Subways, and 327 Starbucks (all as of 2018, according to a report by the Center for an Urban Future[28]). According to the bill's proponents 2700 small businesses will receive relief, including 1800 that will cease paying the tax. While a step in the right direction this doesn't accomplish nearly enough. The unspoken assumption behind the logic of the commercial tax bill is that landlords are sacrosanct. This is an idea that must be challenged. There is no inherent reason to label rezonings that increase property values resulting in skyrocketing rent and commercial homogeneity as "development," as if the process is a sort of scientific law. Like with gentrification in general, corporate and political rhetoric often frame a bipolar choice between urban blight and corporate blandness. Such logic needn't be accepted.

One bill that has sat in the city legislature for quite a long while is the Small Business Jobs Survival Act (SBJSA). This bill pertains to commercial lease renewals. It would give commercial tenants a right to a minimum 10-year lease with a right to renewal, an option for binding arbitration if terms for renewals cannot be agreed upon, and restrictions to prevent landlords from passing property taxes on to small business tenants. DeBlasio championed the SBJSA when he ran for public advocate but has since clammed up about it as mayor, bowing to the real estate industry. Eviction warrants for small businesses haven't abated in the least during de Blasio's first years as mayor. Council Speaker Mark-Viverito had an identical reversal, as council member she sponsored SBJSA but withdrew her support as speaker.

The SBJSA would be another positive but limited step. Landmarking could be expanded to protect significant cultural businesses. That could have saved sites like The Lenox Lounge in Harlem and punk rock mecca CBGBs in the Bowery. San Francisco has a law that requires large stores with more than 11 locations worldwide to get a special permit from the city before moving into any of the city's commercial districts. The conditional use permits cost tens of thousands of dollars and take 4-to-6 months to acquire. The entire point is to make commercial districts less attractive to multinational corporations (banks are unfortunately exempt from the law in San Francisco, something other cities can at least modify).

The truest solution is a return to commercial rent control. This existed in New York City from 1945 to 1963. The law was passed by the state legislature at the behest of then Mayor LaGuardia as a response to exuberant real estate speculation during World War II. The law set a cap on rent increases for any commercial tenant. It was eventually allowed to expire. Its return now can be considered overdue. The de Blasio administration has been dismissive thus far, even as the city tirelessly promotes local neighborhoods to tourists. However, a serious movement for commercial rent control is not beyond the pale of possibility.

Chapter 4

It is not clear how or when East 57th Street and its surrounding environ acquired the name "Billionaire's Row." A decent guess is that it spawned as a marketing tool out of the city's powerful real estate industry. Or perhaps it simply entered into the city's collective consciousness when it became clear the title just fit. It is hardly original even for the general area. A century ago a different angle of Central Park, along 5th Avenue north of 50th Street, inspired the name Millionaire's Row. The Astors, Vanderbilts, and Whitneys built their mansions along the park's edge. Andrew Carnegie would put a 64-room palatial home at 91st Street.

For today's masters of the universe along Billionaire's Row, it isn't exactly mansions, though that description could be subjective; it is rather ultra-luxury apartments reaching the clouds and costing $8000 per square foot that are all the rage. Indeed as of this writing five of the ten tallest buildings in New York have been completed in the past 4 years. Though tall enough to block out the sun in Central Park, many are skinny enough to fit within a few lots. Activists protesting a distortion of the skyline, calling for the city to revisit building codes that couldn't have foreseen the technological advances, like superstrong concrete and new wind-testing, that enable such construction, have thus far hit a wall. City Planning Commissioner Carl Weisbrod was quoted in 2016 in the *New York Times* regarding the selling of air rights for the towers: "This leads to a more interesting streetscape and pedestrian experience as well as an incredibly dynamic iconic skyline that is the envy of the world."

If the rebuilt One World Trade Center holds the top spot for tallest building for the time being it will have close company from the forthcoming 111 West 57th Street, the Steinway Tower, that will top out at a planned 1,438 feet. Down the block stands

One57. At 1,005 feet it has the distinction of being the tallest mixed-use (the 92 apartments stand atop a hotel operated by Hyatt) skyscraper in the city. For several years it held the record sale for an American home sale – Dell Founder Michael Dell paid $100.4 million for the penthouse. A short walk east along 57th street and one encounters the 1,396-foot 432 Park, as of this writing the tallest residential building in the Western Hemisphere. Designed by Rafael Viñoly, it's probably the most architecturally intriguing tower thus far – at 93 feet wide, it's 15 times as tall as wide. According to Viñoly he got his inspiration from a garbage can. Residents here enjoy heated bathroom floors, a private restaurant, and a 75-foot pool and massage therapy room. The first apartment sale went for a reported $18.1 million. Of the more than two dozen properties in the city that closed for more than $30 million in 2016, about half were at 432 Park.

An even skinnier giant tower, Central Park Tower (or Nordstrom Tower) will reach 1550 feet, though its original design featured a spire that was to deliberately leave the tower's peak a single foot shorter than One WTC . It was designed by Adrian Smith and Gordon Gill, the architects that designed the Burj Khalifa in Dubai, currently the tallest building in the world (soon to be displaced by the Jeddah Tower in Saudi Arabia, another Gill and Smith project). Right across the street, at over 900 feet, stands 220 Central Park South. In January 2019 headlines blared that the sale of this tower's penthouse obliterated One57's record: Ken Griffin, founder of the hedge fund Citadel, paid $238 million. Apparently, the penthouse is 34 times bigger than the average Manhattan apartment.

Not far on 60th Street will feature 520 Park whose webpage proclaims "54 stories of Indiana Limestone" with features such as "a classically landscaped private garden with decorative fountains," "an elegant salon, lobby and pool," "3-8 bedroom mansions in the sky." Over on 12th Avenue, along the Hudson River in Hell's Kitchen, stands the completed "VIA 57 West," the

35-story, 709-unit pyramid structure (or perhaps tetrahedron) designed by Bjarke Ingels Group, the Danish architectural firm. Featuring angular balconies that surround an integrated courtyard (according to Bjarke Ingels the green oasis has the same proportions as Central Park but 13,000 times smaller), it's perhaps the chicest of the street's new buildings. While 20 percent of the pyramid's units are labeled affordable, often a slippery label in New York, the remaining will surely fetch a healthy price. The 1000 plus feet 53W53, or MoMA Tower, on 53rd Street will add another looming specter to the skyline. Further downtown, the vicinity of Grand Central Station will soon be graced with the 1,401-foot One Vanderbilt, the result of a de Blasio rezoning of the strip of Vanderbilt Avenue in exchange for $220 million in transportation improvements from developer SL Green.

If the urban ideal is Jane Jacob's sidewalk ballet of seemingly random moving parts making an operatic whole, the present reality is about the polar opposite. One thing that separates today's Billionaire's Row from the older millionaire's row is that the new buildings are not marketed exclusively for New Yorkers, or even Americans. The targeted clientele is the rootless global elite that in the wake of the Great Recession, sees urban real estate as a safe place to park its fortunes. Charles Moore, a former editor of the *Telegraph*, has said that London's property market has become "a form of legalized international money laundering." The infamous Patriot Act, rammed through Congress in the wake of the 9/11 attacks, required that banks, securities houses, and other financial firms follow stringent anti-money-laundering rules. Real estate and escrow agents were to be included but a loophole allowed the Treasury Department to temporarily exempt the real estate industry from the requirements. Indeed, in February 2015, the *New York Times* published a series of stories on the grotesque looking Time Warner Center, just over on Columbus Circle, a short walk from the other towers and essentially a precursor to them. The *Times* revealed that 37 percent of the Center's condominiums are owned by foreigners and at least 16 foreigners who have owned apartments in the building have been the subject of government inquires, either personally or as heads of companies. Four owners had been arrested and another four fined for activities ranging from financial fraud to environmental violations.[1]

Among the characters listed in the *Times* story are Russian oligarch Vitaly Malkin, who for a time was denied entry to Canada for alleged ties to organized crime, and Indian mining magnate Anil Agarwal, accused by an Indian Supreme Court of dumping tons of arsenic around his factory in Tamil Nadu. The reason it falls on investigative journalism to pull back the shade on such transactions is the widespread use of shell companies, known as limited liability companies (LLCs). Primarily first used in the 1970s by oil and gas traders in the Midwest to shield owners from taxation and liability, LLCs have become a common practice in concealing ownership of big money real estate investments. According to the *Times*, shell company ownership accounts for 64 percent of Time Warner Center ownership; for One57 the number has reached 77 percent; 69 percent for The Plaza, 57 for Trump International and Bloomberg Tower.

In a report titled *Hidden in Plain Sight: New York Just Another Island Haven*[2], the International Consortium of Investigative Journalists describe how some of a $6 million-dollar bribe to the wife of former Taiwanese president Chen Shui-bian (the bribe was paid when Chen was serving his second term) ended up in New York. The money went from a bank vault in Taipei to seven suitcases stored in the basement of the corporate executive for whom the bribe was intended to grease through a merger, to banks in Hong King, the US and to a Swiss account before being wired into an account in Miami from where a chunk of it was used to buy a $1.575 apartment in the Onyx Chelsea building, not far from Madison Square Garden.

If hints of money laundering paint too broad a brush, after all celebrities and other wealthy people may desire privacy for understandable reasons, developer Michael Stern, of One57, put it more gently: "The global elite is basically looking for a safe deposit box." According to data put together by the firm PropertyShark, since 2008 about 30 percent of condo sales in large Manhattan developments have been to buyers who have listed either overseas addresses or bought through LLCs.[3] Elsewhere in the city saw a Russian fertilizer oligarch drop $80 million for a condo and Egyptian construction magnate Nassef Sawiris $70 million on a co-op. While these buys draw the most attention there has also been plenty of foreign money flowing toward lower-priced properties.

In what could be seen as his fitting parting shot to the city, former mayor Michael Bloomberg told the *New York Times* in 2013 that, "If we could find a bunch of billionaires around the world to move here, that would be a godsend. Because that's where the revenue comes to take care of everybody else." If that is truly the "Bloombergian" vision for the city it fails, perhaps purposely, to take into account the enticement that draws the said billionaires. While anonymous wealth may at least be the victim of muckraking scorn in the London press, in New York it is greeted with supercheap property taxes and abatements. Thanks in part to an arcane tax code, which much like the building codes, couldn't have foreseen the current boom, owners in the new towers pay significantly less in property taxes than their posh addresses would suggest.

It works this way[4]: property taxes are accessed in three steps. First, properties are classified into one of four classes. Class 1 properties are one-to-three family homes. These properties are responsible for most of the market value of the city's properties (46 percent), but only around 15 percent of the property tax share. Class 3 properties are utility, or industrial. Class 4 is mainly commercial. The towers fall under Class 2 – co-ops, large apartment buildings, large condos, etc.

Second, property market values are estimated by the Department of Finance (DOF). Third is the calculation of a property's assessed value, which is equal to a property's estimated market value multiplied by the applicable target assessment ration. For Class 1 housing the department estimates a property's value by looking at comparable property sales from the previous year. The target assessment is 6 percent (as opposed to the other three classes with a 45 percent target ratio). In order to provide taxpayer relief the assessed value of Class 1 properties cannot grow more than 6 percent in a single year or more than 20 percent over 5 years.

Class 2 can be quite murky. The DOF views properties in Class 2 as if they were income-generating and estimates the market values using the income they generate. Yet owner occupied condos and co-ops don't generate any income so the city uses a two-step process that identifies a comparable rental building (similar size, age, location, etc.) and uses that building's rent roll to draw up an imagined income statement for the building it is accessing. The problem is that when it comes to the new breed of billionaire towers there are simply no comparable rental apartment buildings. Therefore the valuation method ends up grossly undervaluing the properties leading to, as Max Galka explains on the blog Metrocosm, the owner of a $100 million penthouse on One57 having an annual tax bill of only $17,000 a year, a rate of 0.017 percent. Metrocosm listed, as of April 2015, the ten most expensive condos sold in New York showing that if taxed at just the national average of 1.29 percent their tax bill would be a combined $8.7 million a year. However, in reality they pay less than $1 million.[5] Ken Griffin's property tax valuation for his $238 million penthouse of excess came to $9.4 million, or .22 percent of the sales price.[6]

It goes back to 1981 when the state passed a bill resetting property taxes. The bill contained two strange provisions. One prohibited using similar condo sales as a method of accessing value (like the city does for Class 1 properties). The other said that the sum of assessed values of condos within a building could not exceed the assessed value of the whole building. In other words, regardless of location, design, view, floor, if there are 50 units in a $50 million building, the assessment in each unit is capped at $1 million. If such a policy was at least a somewhat justifiable response to the city losing population in the 1970s (though it seemed to beg for gentrification), it is woefully inadequate for the present day.

Then there is the infamous 421-a tax exemption. Another leftover from the 1970s (1971), it gives most newly constructed housing development in the city eligibility for an exemption on property taxes, often up to 25 years. The abatement starts with a steep 95 percent discount slowly decreasing until the tax hits the full rate. As New York's real estate market rebounded in the 1980s, the city designated an "exclusion zone" in Manhattan between 14th and 96th streets that limited the exemption only to developers that built a percentage of affordable units either on- or off-site (off-site being a different property than the one getting the exemption). This was extended to other high demand neighborhoods, though new housing in poorer neighborhoods could qualify without affordable units. The program has been much maligned as being a gift to developers and with good reason: a study by the Independent Budget Office back in 2003 found that from 1985-2002 only 7 percent of the 69,000 subsidized units were affordable to low or moderate-income families. During the Bloomberg years that followed, with their rampant rezoning, affordable units were only 1.7 percent of housing growth between 2005 and 2013. In 2013, the program cost the city just over $1 billion for 150,000 apartments with only 12,748 labeled affordable. When One57's penthouse sold for $100 million, protestors faced off with wary police over its 95 percent tax break (an estimated $360,000). For its part, the real estate industry predictably claims that land and construction costs in New York have become so expensive, which even if true may be the result of decades of subsidization to begin with, that without serious tax breaks rentals could not be built.

Plus there is the issue of corruption and bureaucratic indifference. An October 2016 report by independent newsroom ProPublica reveals that up to two-thirds of the more than 6000 rental properties that receive benefits under 421-a don't have approved applications on file and haven't registered rent-stabilized apartments as required by law[7]. These landlords collectively save $300 million a year in property taxes, pocketing the discount while they wait for the city to approve the benefits they already receive. On the other side, most of these landlords haven't registered their rent-stabilized properties, allowing them to claim they can raise rents as they please. From the city's end the problem is administered by two agencies: The DOF and the Department of Housing, Preservation and Development. The problem is the DOF allows landlords to receive the benefit even though applications haven't been cleared by Housing. Housing in turn allows applications to sit unapproved for years (ProPublica found some dating back to the 1990s, with over 2000 still pending from 2000-10).

Recent media reports have suggested that perhaps, given the sputtering economies in Russia and China, the market of foreign money in New York real estate is cooling. Late in 2015, the Chinese government began more vigilantly enforcing a law forbidding the annual transfer of more than $50,000 a person (according to the National Association of Realtors, Chinese buyers pumped $286 billion into US real estate over the previous year). Here in the US, the Treasury Department began a 6-month initiative requiring real estate companies to disclose names behind cash transactions in Manhattan (for sales over $3 million) and Miami-Dade County (over $1 million). Global oil prices remain low and Britain's vote to leave the European Union has increased volatility. Other global cities have followed suit. Meanwhile, in February 2018, the British Columbia Finance Minister Carole James announced measures targeting foreign buyers and speculators, the flashpoint being Vancouver. Foreigners now have to pay a 20 percent tax on top of the listing value (up from 15 percent), and a levy on property speculators was introduced later that year. Starting that fall, foreign and domestic investors who didn't pay income tax in the province where they owned property started paying a tax of 0.5 percent of the property's assessed value in 2018 and 2 percent thereafter. Home sales dropped in Vancouver to the lowest levels in decades.[8] The UK government overhauled stamp duty land tax rates in 2014, increasing the tax on homes costing more than $1.4 million. New Zealand banned most property sales to non-resident buyers.

On July 11, 2016, the *New York Times* reported that full-floor apartments at 432 Park, originally listed for $78 to $85 million have been split in two and priced at $40 million while developers of 111 West 57th Street will be postponing marketing materials for the building for a year[9]. The glut has continued through 2018: from January through September 2018, inventory in the top 10 percent of Manhattan's apartment market increased by 27.2 percent, while the number of closed sales fell by 11.3 percent.[10] According to a report by real estate company Douglas Elliman, in the last quarter of 2018 the median price for a Manhattan apartment sunk below $1 million to $999,999, the first time that had happened since it crossed the threshold in 2015.[11]

Such mechanisms aren't the only thing undermining Bloomberg's vision of a billionaire city. There's the sheer rootlessness of the world's billionaires. Many of the said billionaires may spend a nice amount on theater tickets and fine dining but many, in addition to paying minimal property taxes, pay no income taxes. Data from the Census Bureau's 2012 American Community Survey revealed 57 percent of apartments in the three-block stretch from East 56th Street to East 59th Street, between Fifth Avenue and Park Avenue, are vacant at least 10 months a year. From East 59th Street to East 63rd Street the vacancy rate is almost 50 percent. Stretching it out further, the Bureau estimates that 30 percent of all apartments in the entire quadrant from East 49th to East 70th streets are vacant at least 10 months a year[12]. It turns out Billionaire's Row is a playground that is deserted most of the time.

As New York's symbolic center is used for real estate speculation and second (or third) homes for the very rich, the housing situation in the rest of the city is less than pristine. In October 2015 the office of New York City Comptroller Scott Stringer released a report titled *Hidden Households* that found overcrowding, an established predictor of homeless and overall indicator of poor health and safety, has risen in recent years. The report found that the city's overall crowded rate was 8.8 percent, a proportional increase of 15.8 percent from 2005-13. That is more than two-and-a-half times the national rate of 3.3 percent. Severe overcrowding, characterized as housing units with more than 1.5 persons per room, increased even more: 44.8 percent over the same period[13]. A November 2015 report by the Citizen's Budget Commission found that 42 percent of renters are burdened – spending more than a third of their income on rent; half of those burdened are severely burdened, spending more than half their income.

The real estate market has reached such a plateau that the spring of 2016 saw the opening of Carmel Place in Midtown, New York's first complex of "micro-apartments"; meant to appeal to the hordes of single adults that have come to dominate images of modern urban living, these apartments range from 260 to 360 square feet. Back in 1987, the city passed a law forbidding the construction of apartments smaller than 400 square feet. Such apartments were known as Single Room Occupancies (SROs) and while they were a source of affordable housing, they had fallen out of repair and esteem by the mid-1980s. The law was waived by Bloomberg for the 55 units at Carmel Place. A total of 14 of the units will be designated affordable, going for either $950 dollars or $1490, the rest, which will come with Wi-Fi, cable, and weekly cleaning, range from $2400 to $2900. Touted as a possible solution to New York's affordable housing problem, the first micro-apartments ironically boast some of the highest prices per square foot in the city – clearly not the greatest of deals. Still some housing advocates argue that perhaps "micro-luxury" is a better foothold for the concept given the stigma attached to SROs for the poor.

Such a market gone mad is the impetus for the housing plan put forward by Mayor de Blasio, the proclaimed goal of which is the preservation and building of 200,000 affordable units. The distinction between preserving and building is worth noting, especially as the former appears to be the greater number under de Blasio's plan, though building would seem to be the more ambitious initiative. This comes, though, after three terms of Bloomberg's "luxury product" and the previous terms of Giuliani's nonexistent housing policy. During Giuliani's time only 75,000 units of new housing were built (compared for instance to 300,000 new units during the 1960s under mayors Wagner and Lindsay). A report from NYU's Furman Center for Real Estate and Urban Policy classified city neighborhoods by three categories: gentrifying, non-gentrifying, and higher-income. Of the 55 neighborhoods classified in the report only seven were labeled non-gentrifying[14]. Four of the neighborhoods are in the Bronx – Highbridge, University Heights, and Parkchester in the South Bronx, Kingsbridge Heights in the northwest, and three in Brooklyn – Coney Island, Bensonhurst, and East New York, though East New York figures in the crosshairs as the first neighborhood targeted under de Blasio's plan (see below). A total of 33 neighborhoods were labeled high-income while 15 were labeled gentrifying. The gentrifying category, defined as neighborhoods with low-income in 1990 that experienced rent growth above the median sub-borough areas (SBA) rent growth between 1990 and 2014, featured many of the neighborhoods one would expect. Greenpoint/Williamsburg predictably was the most gentrified area seeing a whopping 78.7 percent rent increase from 1990 to 2004 and it was joined by nearby neighborhoods in Northern Brooklyn, namely Bushwick, a 44 percent increase, and Bedford-Stuyvesant, at 36.1 percent. According to the blog StreetEasy, the median income-to-rent ratio, which measures the share of income spent on median market rent, in Williamsburg is an astounding 85.9 percent, in Bushwick 80.1. Central and East Harlem were also high on the list, Central Harlem posting an increase of 50 percent, East Harlem 40.3. Nearby Morningside Heights saw a 36.7 increase. Of course, the Lower East Side's increase was more than 50 percent while in Queens Astoria saw a jump of almost 30 percent.

New York, of course, is a city of renters, accounting for two-thirds of the population, a fact often praised by libertarian types for giving the city's labor force a good amount of flexibility; however this can be at least somewhat attributable to the costs of homeownership whether in the form of co-ops, condos, or one-to-three family homes. In 2014 the average sale price of such forms of ownership in the city was $575,700, limiting the option to only the top quarter of income, particularly in a time of tight credit. In Brooklyn a median priced home currently takes up 98 percent of the borough's median income – meaning a typical household would have to use almost its entire monthly income for a monthly mortgage. According to the firm RealtyTrac that makes Brooklyn the most unaffordable city for home ownership, while Manhattan (95 percent) and the Bronx (82 percent) were third and fourth on that list (San Francisco listed second with 97.44 percent).

De Blasio's housing plan, classified under the banner of "mandatory inclusionary housing," targets 15 neighborhoods beginning with East New York, and proposes changes in local zoning that would allow developers the right to build bigger buildings in exchange for a certain percentage of units reserved as affordable. Under the plan as originally proposed, the council would have three options for each particular rezoning: 25 percent of new apartments to rent for an average of about $1,165 a month for people making 60 percent of the metropolitan area's median income (AMI), about $36,000 for an individual and $51,780 for a family of four; 30 percent renting for an average of $1,580 for people making 80 percent of AMI, about $62,000 for a family of three; 30 percent for households at 120 percent of AMI renting at a higher $2300 – this option for so called "emerging markets"; i.e., neighborhoods already gentrifying. That last option would be available south of 96th Street on the East Side and south of 110th Street on the West Side. The rezonings would be concentrated at major transit points, including East Harlem, Washington Heights, parts of Flushing, the Jerome Avenue corridor in the Bronx, and Long Island City in Queens.

Upon passing the overall plan in March, the council added a fourth option, the one that will apply to East New York: 20 percent of units at 40 percent of AMI, or roughly $31,000 a year and a lowering of the affordability cap from 120 to 115 percent of AMI. Another revision is an additional 5 percent of affordable units if the units are built off-site (the mayor also agreed, at the urging of activists, to conduct a study of the neighborhoods slated for rezoning). At least before that revision the housing plan was rejected by four of the five borough presidents and 50 of 59 community boards. Developers, of course, will have the ultimate say in what mix of affordability will be included in their projects.

A few weeks later on April 20, 2016 the city council overwhelmingly and unsurprisingly approved the plan for East New York. The final tally was 45-1-0. Perhaps it is equally unsurprising that the plan has received the endorsement of the *New York Times*. In a recent op-ed that was titled "Saving a New York Neighborhood From Gentrification," the *Times* basically bought City Hall's line, while acknowledging that it is "paradoxical," "that gentrification is coming anyway, that people are already proclaiming East New York as the next Williamsburg. Without a strict zoning plan, East New York will not be spared."

Of course, it is not at all difficult to posit obvious objections to such sentiments. Even given the percentage of apartments labeled affordable, how exactly would thousands of what passes for market rate units in the city these days limit gentrification in the greater neighborhood (overall the plan calls for just over 6000 new apartments by 2030)? Such a system, given local changes that figure to result, may well accelerate it. And there is the question of AMI. The metropolitan area's median calculation includes higher-income areas in Long Island and Westchester that bring the median into the upper half of the city's median. In the case of East New York, 53 percent of the neighborhood's residents make less than $35,000 a year but would seem to only receive 13 percent of the planned housing while more than half would go to the 14 percent of residents making $75,000. In the Jerome Avenue corridor, the median income of $25,000 is less than 33 percent of AMI. In East Harlem the median income of $28,000 is 37 percent of AMI.

The administration claims that 40 percent of the affordable units in East New York will go to incomes between $23,000-38,000. Even taking the reforms issued by the city council, which also include a plan for an expedited 1,300 affordable units over the next few years and scaling back of proposed industrial zoning changes, there is still plenty of room for high-end development – a fact that the market has recognized with fast rising land prices in the neighborhood. Brother Paul Mohammad of the Coalition for Community Advancement succinctly declared (quoted in *The Gothamist*) "the first plan was arsenic and this one is just a watered down version of the poison."

The administration claims it can alleviate the AMI issue by further subsidizing developers on individual projects within the general housing plan. The extreme inefficiency of this approach can be clearly seen in the case of Stuyvesant Town, the massive apartment complex on the East Side. Built in 1947 by Metropolitan Life, then the largest corporation in the country, in partnership with the city led by Robert Moses, in an effort to bring a suburban aura to the city – thousands of working-class tenements were cleared from the site, though by most accounts there were no large protests and the area's population had dropped in the years prior to the clearing. Stuy Town for decades was held, despite its haunting architecture, as a paragon of middle-class housing in the city. Many of its original white-only inhabitants were veterans just returned from World War II.

For decades its rent stabilized, 11,232 apartments were a solid investment for Met Life, reporting a net operating income of $112 million in 2006. However, with Met Life becoming a publicly-traded company in the mid-2000s shareholders demanded more. The waiting list for affordable apartments was closed and regulations began to be lifted. In 2006 came the disastrous $5.4 billion sale to Tishman Speyer and Blackrock Realty. The sale was financed almost entirely with leveraged debt, debt that was quickly securitized and sold to other investors.

The immediate problem was that rental income from Stuy Town only covered about 40 per cent of the debt load. This led to the requisite squeezing and harassment of tenants. In October 2009 the New York State Court of Appeals ruled that Tishman Speyer and Met Life wrongly deregulated 4,440 apartments and ordered compensation. The group defaulted on $4.4 billion in loans in January 2010 (though the main hit was taken by Fannie Mae and Freddie Mac – $2 billion, along with other investors including the Church of England and government of Singapore).

In October of 2015, the complex was sold to the Blackstone Group, the country's largest landlord, a sale helped along by the de Blasio administration. By now half of the complex's units have been deregulated commanding $4,200 a month for two bedrooms on the open market. The deal with Blackstone guarantees a more affordable rate for the other half for 20 years. Besides owning a gigantic piece of Manhattan real estate what does Blackstone get in exchange for this bit of philanthropy? A total of $221 million in city funding – $77 million in tax breaks and a 20-year $144 million self-amortizing loan structured to basically function as another city subsidy, and, even more significant, city support for transferring Stuy Town's unused air rights to properties elsewhere in the city.

Air rights refer to empty space above a building. If, for example, a neighborhood is zoned for a limit of 35 stories and a building stands at five stories, the leftover potential space can be sold to another owner enabling that owner to build a taller property, above the 35-story limit. Normally the properties selling air rights must be adjacent. An owner needs to buy the air rights of a next-door neighbor before buying any others, then the next neighbor's and so on. The Stuy Town complex, 110 buildings spread out over 80 acres with more than 1 million square feet of unused air rights, presents quite a bonanza, particularly if the air rights can be applied in other parts of Manhattan. Extremely valuable air rights and $221 million in extra funding all in exchange for keeping half a complex worth of apartments labeled affordable. Thus the de Blasio administration declared victory.

A similar dynamic was involved with the Riverton housing complex in Harlem, another project built by Met Life in 1947 (initially it was built to stem any criticism about the segregation of Stuyvesant Town). After years of uncertainty, again due to a previous buyer being saddled with debt that was to be cleared by displacing longstanding residents, the 1,229-unit complex was sold to Douglas Eisenberg of A&E Real Estate Holdings for $201 million in a deal with the city that is supposed to keep 975 units affordable to middle and working-class residents for 30 years. In exchange, the city is giving tax breaks and incentives worth $100 million over that period (including $92 in property tax exemptions).

Such is the inevitable result of accepting gentrification as a simple fact of life and relying exclusively on private sector solutions, something the *Times* certainly didn't question. Such policies need big developers to be on board and that means fairer proposals, even within the same context, such as a 50-50 split between market rate and affordable housing can be dismissed as not profitable enough and threatening housing production, and where there are developers there are waiver requests, exemptions, and non-enforcement (a hallmark of the Bloomberg years in New York and in other cities are buyouts that allow developers to simply pay a set amount upfront to get out of putting aside any affordable units. De Blasio's plan seems to at least avoid that). A study published in *City Limits* last November showed that developers can expect to achieve a yield of 8.7 percent under the first option of the plan. For its part the administration claimed to build or preserve 6,844 affordable apartments in 2016. Smarting from criticism that these apartments aren't reaching the poorest people, 20 percent of these apartments are alleged to have been earmarked for households earning less than $25,000 a year.

It also speaks to the city's reliance on zoning. Zoning, or rezoning, rather than planning, has long been the city's method of choice. During the Bloomberg years some 37 percent of the city's land was rezoned. Rezonings generally fall into three categories: upzoning, increasing development capacity (i.e. larger buildings), downzonings that preserve existing capacity, and hybrids that are a mix of both.

Perhaps somewhat contrary to Bloomberg's pro-growth agenda, many of the rezonings under his watch were to some extent of the preserving kind. Predictably studies have shown that lots downzoned tended to be in neighborhoods that had higher incomes and rates of homeownership. This was especially true for hybrid rezonings. A Furman Center study found upzonings were in neighborhoods with significantly lower income and homeownership rates. In other words, poorer neighborhoods are targeted for gentrification while neighborhoods full of homeowners have enough clout to get preservation (usually in low density neighborhoods where greater density would be an environmental improvement). Needless to say in such a system racial minorities receive the brunt of displacement.[15]

Brooklyn was a main target. In 2003 Park Slope saw an upzoning along Fourth Avenue, this one had no inclusionary housing mandate. A few years later in 2012 hundreds more brownstones were added to the thousands that have been part of the historic district (i.e. protected from redevelopment) since the early 1970s. The neighborhood currently has the largest historic district in the city.

There was the 2004 rezoning of Downtown Brooklyn. Originally proclaimed by planners as an effort to increase office space, a June 2001 report by a committee organized by Senator Charles Schumer, dubbed the "Group of 35," called for 60 million square feet of new commercial space by 2020 in response to a perceived lack of office space during the dot-com boom of the late 1990s. From the beginning the process was dominated by City Hall and closely aligned business groups starting with the Downtown Brooklyn Council (later becoming the Downtown Brooklyn Partnership). The rezoning was approved by the city council with only one abstention.

As it turned out there wasn't a crisis of office space. In fact, Metrotech, a nearby business complex (itself a product of an earlier subsidized urban renewal plan to bring office space downtown), lost both JP Morgan Chase and Empire Blue Cross in 2006 leaving about 350,000 open square feet of space. If there was no great need for office space, developers had no trouble finding a highly profitable alternative: luxury condos. Indeed, the tallest buildings now in Brooklyn are all brand new and located downtown. There's the 610-foot 750 apartment units building known as The Hub on Schermerhorn Street, AVA DoBro over on Willoughby Street, The Brooklyner right down the block, 388 Bride Street. Earlier in 2016 headlines screamed of the newly approved plans for a 1,066-foot skyscraper apartment building at 340 Flatbush Avenue Extension. As for all the projected office space, the original plan projected 4.6 million square feet of commercial development – less than 30 percent has turned up according to analysis by Brooklyn Borough President Eric Adams, while expecting 979 apartments instead of the 11,000 developed or coming.

As we saw in Chapter One, in 2005 it was Williamsburg's turn for rezoning. The most visible effect of this rezoning, which was put into effect over an earlier community developed plan that had approval of the City Planning Committee, has been the explosion of high-rise luxury apartments that have all but finished off industry along the East River waterfront (the rezoning preserved miniscule sections of industry in the area, others were zoned as mixed – either industry or residential; however most owners converted to higher profit residential use).

Harlem saw the same kind of thing after its rezonings. First there was the 2003 rezoning of Frederick Douglas Boulevard, a plan that increased residential capacity in the targeted area's 44 blocks by 50 percent, then there was the 2009 125th Street Corridor. The impact of the rezonings, along with the expansion of Columbia University, has been clear; along with the familiar mushrooming of high-end condos and boutiques, the population of Central Harlem grew by 9 percent in a decade, its black population falling by 12 percent while its white population increased by over 400 percent. Meanwhile East Harlem, long known as El Barrio, is facing a huge potential upzoning covering 96 blocks from Fifth to Second avenues, from 104th to 132nd streets.

A cynical chorus may sing that worries about gentrification are needless since surely East New York could use a healthy dose of it. After all, even during times of high crime East New York stood out as among the poorest and most violent neighborhoods in the city. Today it ranks on top in total number of murders (though its murder rate is lower than Ocean Hill and Brownsville, nearby neighborhoods). Like the South Bronx, for a long time East New York served as a symbol of urban decay, though unlike the South Bronx its wreckage wasn't captured for posterity by Howard Cosell nor did East New York have the honor of a presidential visit. East New York has until recently been a ghetto even more hidden.

The origins of East New York go back to a Dutch settlement in the late seventeenth century. The name "East New York" came from Connecticut merchant John Pitkin who arrived in 1835 with ambitions to turn the farming community into a center of urban commerce. Pitkin purchased 135 acres and named his territory East New York to clearly demonstrate the scope of what he had in mind. While the Panic of 1837 would wipe out Pitkin's plans, though Pitkin Avenue remains a prominent thoroughfare, the development of New York's infrastructure, its subways and trolley lines, and waves of European immigration would gradually populate the area. The 1901 Tenement House Law, requiring fire escapes, access to light, and improved sanitary conditions for new tenements helped to spur many to flee the older tenement districts like the Lower East Side. East New York became a diverse mix of Germans, Italians, Poles, and Jews (the Jewish population became especially significant in next-door Brownsville).

If East New York could fairly be described as a solid working-class neighborhood up through the mid-1960s, it would soon after fall victim to a toxic brew of the poor urban planning, neglect, and racism we saw in other neighborhoods. Urban planner Walter Thabit opens his book *How East New York became a Ghetto* with the following, echoing the histories of Bushwick and the South Bronx:

> The Central part of East New York in Brooklyn, home to 100,000 people in 1965, was largely destroyed in the following decade. The destruction accompanied a racial shift in the population, from 85 percent white in 1960 to 80 percent black and Puerto Rican by 1966. During that period, the racially biased policies of real estate brokers and speculators...the redlining of the community by the banks, and almost total neglect of the situation by the city and its agencies brought the area to the brink of collapse.[16]

Blockbusters and real estate hustlers filled the neighborhood provoking white flight, helped along by subsidized suburbanization and white racism, and black residents, denied housing opportunities elsewhere in the city and exploited by the same real estate interests, channeled into a neighborhood that, redlined by banks, immediately faced a shortage of services and a stagnant local economy. As East New York filled with thousands of children, and the Catholic schools that had served the neighborhood's previous population closed, the Board of Education was unable or unwilling to build a single new school. As Thabit documents, at its worst a third of East New York's children were getting less than a full day of schooling from the late 1960s to the early 1970s. Isolated public housing (also pronounced in Brownsville) further segregated poverty. The predictable ghetto that resulted from all this was ripe to descend into violence, particularly during the crack epidemic of the late 1980s-early 1990s.

Now with the crack epidemic in the past, New York branding itself as "the safest big city in the world," and gentrification, much of it a direct result of city policy, East New York finds itself, along with Brownsville, billed as a sort of final frontier in Brooklyn real estate. As has happened in neighborhoods throughout the city, longtime residents who endured the worst of times and rebuilt their communities now face the prospect of their neighborhoods being sold out from under them. Whereas ghettoization once expanded to East New York, from neighborhoods such as Bedford-Stuyvesant now comes gentrification. Whereas once blockbusters fanned out to drain the lifeblood of the community, now along come speculative vampires. A January 2015 story in *New York Magazine* counted nearly 700 instances of house-flipping in East Brooklyn in the previous two years, in East New York specifically such houses affected 7.3 percent of neighborhood houses with an average price increase on resale of 143.7 percent.[17]

The city council did reject a de Blasio supported rezoning for Inwood (in northern Manhattan) that would have allowed a 15-story development that was to be the first individual building project under the mayor's plan. A groundswell of opposition from residents protesting that the affordable units under the plan were inadequate forced the local councilperson to reject the project. However, the developers can now build a slightly smaller building at the site without any affordable housing provision. A similar individual project in Sunnyside, Queens was also defeated due to community opposition.

Besides accepting gentrification and relying exclusively on private sector solutions, the city's housing crisis speaks to a city that has shunned comprehensive urban planning in favor of a system of local zoning. This can be said even in a city that saw the epoch of Robert Moses. The lack of planning has deep roots and from the beginning had a timeless enemy: the city's powerful real estate industry. It could be taken back to the beginning when New York was the Dutch settlement New Amsterdam. Its most prominent leader, Peter Stuyvesant, faced chaotic development and ordered all property be surveyed and streets laid out, though Stuyvesant didn't organize a vision for a future city but only tried to rationalize property relations that already existed.

The year 1811 saw Manhattan's infamous grid laid out. Rational to the extreme, avenues running north and south, streets running east and west at countless right angles, the grid has always had its prominent critics. In 1849 Walt Whitman lamented: "Our perpetual dead flat and streets cutting each other at right angles, are certainly the last things in the world consistent with beauty of situation." Henry James hated the city's "primal topographic curse, her old inconceivably bourgeois scheme of composition and distribution, the uncorrected labor of minds with no imagination of the future and blind before the opportunity given them by their two magnificent waterfronts." Edith Wharton was turned off by "rectangular New York...this cramped horizontal gridiron of a town...hidebound in its deadly uniformity of mean ugliness."

The grid fulfilled its purpose of forming uniform blocks that can easily be subdivided and sold, mirroring the dividing of farmland that was taking place before the plan. While the grid succeeded in its development mission, and is perhaps forever appreciated by tourists, it left little room for public squares or parks. The main green exception, Central Park, while iconic, from a housing standpoint serves primarily to greatly raise property values for homes that surround it creating yesterday's Millionaire's Row and today's Billionaire's Row. Central Park also obscures the fact that Manhattan has very few equally necessary smaller, local green spaces completely open to the public.

The first subway opened in October 1904, and though funded with public money to the tune of $35 million, it was built and operated under the direction of August Belmont (Belmont supplied the cars, signals, and other equipment from his own funds) and his Interborough Rapid Transit Company (IRT). If New York's subway is an engineering marvel that opened vast spaces of the city to waves of immigrants and their children, it was built by business interests at a time when the idea of "conflict of interests" was largely foreign. Charles T. Barney, director of IRT in 1900 and one of the city's top speculators, exploited his inside knowledge about the coming subway's route through upper Manhattan to buy up property in Harlem, Washington Heights, and the Bronx, organizing a syndicate commanding $7 million. Belmont himself speculated with land on City Island with the same advance knowledge.

Builders buying that land faced great pressure to develop their property in order to recoup their investment and pay back loans. Predictably they focused on housing that could be built quickly, cheaply, and profitably given the high land costs. That could only have meant tenement expansion. It is true given that the Tenement Law of 1901 required windows in each room, fire escapes, and more open space, that the new tenements in the Bronx were generally considered by the many that moved there an improvement over the squalor of the infamous Lower East Side where it should be noted the original IRT lines (Lines 1-9 of the system) didn't go near due to its lack of open-space speculative opportunities. Yet it's also true that there was much haphazard development and even the tenement reform wasn't applied everywhere. When the Brooklyn Rapid Transit Company's subway opened the eastern part of Brooklyn for development, the speculative nature of neighborhood housing, and the fact that many of the tenements there were too small to be regulated, particularly in Brownsville, was a main cause of the long-term decline of the neighborhood. Real estate types lost interest in the subways by the time the city finally built the IND lines (lines A-G) in the 1930s to serve the earlier developed areas their lines ignored. By then, the real estate industry was looking to cars and highways to serve the purpose the first subways performed.

The city's 1916 Zoning Resolution, the first comprehensive

zoning law in the country, was similar to the grid plan in that it followed rather than led the real estate market. The resolution set up separate residential and business districts (in Manhattan not the outer boroughs) and, in the aftermath of the completion of the grotesque Equitable Building on Broadway, regulated the shape of skyscrapers for the allowance of air and light on sidewalks (the Equitable Building often gets the blame for inspiring the resolution; however the Heights of Building Commission drafted the ordinance 2 years before Equitable was completed). Skyscrapers would have to be "set back," i.e. get skinnier, after reaching a certain height. The particular height required for the set-back depended on the width of the street on which the building was located.

While ostensibly progressive the law also had the support of the real estate community for its concern with property values. Back then businesses often meant factories which meant zoning to separate businesses from homes; by definition this meant keeping the working class away from fashionable shopping avenues that factories were encroaching upon. And as the webpage NYCZoning itself describes the Equitable Building:

> Rising without setbacks to its full height of 538 feet, the Equitable Building cast a seven-acre shadow over neighboring buildings, affecting their value and setting the stage for the nation's first comprehensive zoning resolution.

If the housing situation in New York seems dire it must be acknowledged that there is not much of it that is inevitable. It is oft remarked by boosters that the increased desirability for living in low crime New York is the driver for the high prices of the city's rents and homes. Certainly it is a factor that the city's population has grown by a million people since 1990. Conservatives, as well as the de Blasio administration, see the solution simply through increasing supply, which will surely be part of any solution – even with New York's booming population its population density, though being the highest of any major American city, is considerably less than such cities as Buenos Aires, Warsaw, and Barcelona. Actually worldwide New York's population density wouldn't come close to cracking the world's top 100. Even hipster Brooklyn's settlement is less dense than it was in 1950. Manhattan's own density is less than it was a century ago, granted a century ago downtown was a teeming slum with awful unsanitary conditions, as is much of the world's crowded cities. The point, however, is there is room to comfortably add more volume. New York lags behind other American cities in constructing new housing units. Figures compiled by the Department of Housing and Urban Development show that in 2014 20,483 new housing permits were issued, about 2.4 units for every 1000 people. While a good improvement over the city's building pace from the 1990s (a signal failure of the vaunted Giuliani administration), it is still lower than other cities such as San Francisco (often described as a city where new development is considered impossible, but it saw 3.2 permits per 1000 in 2014), DC (6.4), and Seattle (11.5).

If greater density is in general desirable there is sound reason to think it isn't the main answer to the housing crisis. A 2013 report by the Association for Neighborhood Housing and Development points out:

> From 2000 to 2010, the population of New York increased by 2.1 percent while the US Census reported that the number of occupied housing units increased by more than twice that amount, 5.3 percent. . .If we could build our way out of our affordability crisis, the ratio of housing costs to income should have gone down during this period. However, average rents and the share of income spent on rent both increased well above inflation over the same period.

While with greater demand obviously comes higher prices, the accelerant spreading the madness is investment, whether from billionaire tycoons or local speculators. The fact is that what passes as "market" in New York means luxury apartments, gentrification, and overcrowding. Without regulations or nonmarket housing, greater density in a time of record inequality simply allows greater opportunity for speculation as building for the extremely wealthy offers much greater profits to developers. However, municipalities have access to solutions. A flip tax can be applied to increase state real estate transfer taxes to property that is resold after a short period of time to discourage short-term speculation. The tax code could be reformed to properly tax the new towers dotting the city's skyline. The AMI could be adjusted to be calculated only for New York City rather than including surrounding wealthier areas thereby making the affordable housing under de Blasio's plan actually affordable to any rezoned neighborhoods.

Rent stabilization, or rent control, could be expanded. New York has an extensive system of rent stabilization that goes back a long way, albeit with a labyrinth of loopholes. In 1950 New York State regulated 96 percent of rentals in the city and 80 percent of housing in general. As time went by and the state shed the program, the city and a few other localities maintained some level of it. Basically, rent stabilization applies to buildings built before 1974 with six or more units not including co-ops or condos. The rents for the units could be raised a small percentage every year, as determined by an annual vote by the Rent Guidelines Board (a nine-person body appointed by the mayor) until the rent gets to $2500 and the unit is vacated at which point it can be deregulated and rented at market price. Until recently a tenant's gross annual income cannot legally be more than $200,000 (if a tenant's income does reach over $200,000 and the rent has reached $2700 the unit can be deregulated). To its credit, under the first 2 years of de Blasio's control the Rent Guidelines Board has voted for a rent freeze for the first time in its 46-year history.

Rent stabilization is separate from its grander cousin rent control. Rent control applies to tenants living in buildings built before 1947 who have been living in the unit continuously since 1971. The leases can be passed on to family members who have lived in the unit for 2 years before the holder of the lease passes away. Put in place after World War II to provide for returning soldiers confronting a severe housing shortage, rent-controlled apartments have dwindled from a high of two million in the 1950s to about 27,000, as opposed to over a million rent stabilized (accounting for 47 percent of the city's market). It has been a while since any rent-controlled leases have been drawn up and even the Rent Guidelines Board's webpage declares the long-term trend for such apartments is zero. Conservatives like to market rent control as a cushy giveaway to well-off people; however, figures from the city's 2014 Housing and Vacancy Survey showed the median rent for a rent-controlled apartment that year was $1,050 a month. The median income for a rent-controlled tenant: $29,000. For rent stabilized tenants the median numbers were $1,300 rent and $40,600 income.

If the power of the real estate lobby can be countered, in the last state-level election cycle members of the Real Estate Board of New York and their firms contributed more than 10 percent of the contributions that entered into the campaign finance system, the rent stabilization system can be reformed and expanded, even to cover commercial properties preserving local diversity and limiting the spread of homogenous corporate brands. The deregulation part of the law was only put into effect in 1994. With total repeal of a popular program unlikely decontrol was always a goal of the real estate industry. The law was passed with the justification of denying rent stabilization to wealthy people getting beautiful apartments on the cheap. Granted back in 1994 hardly anyone outside of Manhattan's most fashionable neighborhoods was paying $2000 a month rent; however, politicians seeking campaign money and not being the most prescient lot, the result was that of the 860,000 apartments that were stabilized at the time the law passed, almost 250,000 have become free market units. This is thanks not only to the basic law but also to loopholes that allow for claims of expensive renovations to vacant apartments to justify higher rent, even allowing an increase of 20 percent in rent when stabilized apartments become vacant giving obvious motivation to tenant harassment and fraud.

An August 2017 article in the *New York Review of Books* titled *Tenants Under Siege: Inside New York City's Housing Crisis* lists some instances that reflect countless examples of this harassment:

An artist I know in South Williamsburg took flight after her landlord paid a homeless man to sleep outside her door, defecate in the hallway, invite friends in for drug-fueled parties, and taunt her as she entered and left the building. In East New York a mother tells me of a landlord who, after claiming to smell gas in the hallway, gained entry to her apartment and then locked her out. In January, a couple with a three-month-old baby in Bushwick complained to the city because they had no heat. In response, the landlord threatened to alert the Administration for Children's Services that they were living in an unheated apartment. Fearful of losing their child, they left, leaving the owner with what he wanted: a vacant unit.[18]

The rent limit was raised to $2700 in 2011. In real terms $2000 in 1994 equals $3260 today, thus the raise's effect was minimal. Control over rent stabilization and control can and should be returned from the state to the city's government.

The same is true for public housing. New York has by far the largest public housing system in the United States. Unlike cities such as Chicago and St Louis, New York's public housing still stands, housing over 400,000 tenants (another 230,000 live in

Section 8 housing). From a general perspective public housing has been a mixed bag. From an historical perspective, its housing stock is certainly better than the tenements it replaced. In areas such as the Lower East Side and North Brooklyn, public housing acts as a barrier to homogeny ensuring to some extent local economic and ethnic diversity, one of the pillars of its original vision (perhaps an irony of gentrification in some neighborhoods), while in other places, such as Brownsville, poor planning left public housing stagnant and isolated. New York Housing Authority faces annual operating deficits of tens of millions yet has a waiting list of over 200,000 (more on public housing in Chapter 5).

An idea that may be gaining steam is the implementing or expanding of community land trusts. The basic idea is that a piece of property is owned by a non-profit with a building owned by some form of mutual housing association which can sell or rent apartments for a low cost. Since the land trust owns the land it controls the development, keeping the property outside of gentrification and speculation and ensuring affordability over time.

There are examples of this that have worked. The Cooper Square Mutual Housing Association, with its roots in the Cooper Square Committee's battle against one Robert Moses' planned clearances of buildings between East 9th Street and Delancey Street from the Bowery to 2nd Avenue, was established in 1991 through a hard negotiation with the city. It operates a housing cooperative with over 300 apartments. The NYC Community Land Initiative's webpage (NYCCLI is an alliance of social justice and affordable housing organizations) lists numerous other trusts throughout the country.

A major question is how much available land there is for such community trusts. In February 2016 the Comptroller's Office released a report documenting over 1100 vacant public lots that could possibly be used for affordable housing by being put into a "land bank." For its part the city claims that only 670 of these are suitable to develop and that development plans are ongoing on 400 of them.

Still there are other solid possibilities. Until 1996 the city would foreclose and seize on severely distressed, tax-delinquent properties. Under Giuliani the policy changed and rather than seize the properties the city began, after giving owners a period of 90 days to pay their balance, get on a payment plan, or establish eligibility for an exemption, selling the liens to a private investment trust that hires services to collect the debt while also charging the owner a 9 percent interest rate and assorted fees. While the process can be credited for pressuring owners to pay their property taxes, the delinquent rate has gone down from an average of 4.4 percent in the early 1990s to 1.4 percent in 2014, bringing $1.3 billion to the city's coffers between the sales and more property tax payments, it often leads to homeowners facing predatory interest rates to sell the property to private equity firms. However, with the city's Third Party Transfer (TPT) program tax, delinquent properties can be transferred to "responsible owners." These can be nonprofits and de Blasio's housing plan does include use of TPT (plus there are still almost 900 apartments vacant from the original city ownership program).

A December 2015 report by Picture the Homeless (an organization that is part of the NYCCLI coalition) titled *Banking on Vacancy: Homelessness and Real Estate Speculation* thoroughly describes the speculative practice of warehousing, i.e. keeping property vacant in neighborhoods that are gentrifying or it is figured will do so in the future in order to reap the benefits of expected higher rent or sales prices, or possibly waiting to acquire nearby properties to consolidate with the property kept vacant[19]. As we've seen this extends even to commercial property in well-off downtown neighborhoods like Tribeca and SoHo where any day one can see empty numerous storefronts as the promise of skyrocketing rents has owners, often LLCs, holding out for the promise of renting to a bank branch or banal nation chain. The holdout could leave the property vacant for years. The report estimates that the amount of vacant property in the city could house its exploding homeless population, over 60,000 by official numbers as of this writing, five times over. Some quite sensible reforms the report lists include imposing a 3-year limit for a residential unit to remain without tenants and turning any vacant city owned property, about 10 percent of the total, into low-income housing with low-income people willing to put their own work into any needed repairs granted ownership through the value of their sweat equity (a concept we ran into with the gentrifying pioneers of Brownstone Brooklyn, which is just what it sounds like: "a contribution to a project or enterprise in the form of sweat and toil," as defined by Investopedia. If it was good enough for Brooklyn's early gentrifying pioneers, it can work for poorer people).

In June 2019 tenants won a victory when Governor Cuomo signed legislation passed by a resurgent Democratic majority which repealed the vacancy bonus along with vacancy decontrol when the rent reaches $2774.76 and the unit becomes vacant. Also repealed was the high-income deregulation, when a unit is removed from rent stabilization because the tenant's income is $200,000 or higher for 2 consecutive years. This legislation, while significant, will mainly cover buildings built before 1974. It doesn't figure to add much affordable housing to the city's stock.

Obviously taken individually none of these solutions is a panacea. At bottom it comes down to a question of housing versus real estate. If to many this seems like a lopsided contest, the primacy of private property and such, it should be noted the housing end has much to support it. In the Universal Declaration of Human Rights passed by the UN General Assembly in 1948 it is stated: "Everyone has the right to a standard of living adequate for the health and well-being of himself and of his family, including food, clothing, housing and medical care and necessary social services, and the right to security in the event of unemployment, sickness, disability, widowhood, old age or other lack of livelihood in circumstances beyond his control." The Housing Act passed at home by Congress in 1949 reads the words, "a decent home and a suitable living environment for every American family." Such sentiment seems to go beyond the concept of shelter. Shelter isn't housing. Housing should encompass not only modern, livable conditions but also protection against displacement and the promise of being part of a thriving stable community. In a city largely dominated by real estate interests these laws remain tragically ignored but as long as there have been rents there has been resistance.

The de Blasio administration while loudly touting its housing plan has at the same time tempered expectations. Speaking at a town hall meeting in Bedford-Stuyvesant, a neighborhood facing intensive gentrification pressure, de Blasio warned the attendees not to "think the city is all powerful. This is about something called money." Deputy Mayor for housing and economic development Alicia Glen, an alumni of Goldman Sachs, put it more succinctly in an interview with Peter Moskowitz for his book *How To Kill a City: Gentrification, Inequality, and the Fight for the Neighborhood* saying:

> The reason why so many people are pissed is that they have been conditioned to the fear of change...But change is inevitable and how you shape it is incredibly important as opposed to letting it wash over you. Because it's coming. We have certain tools in our municipal tool box. We can't change the entire history of capitalism and we're not Trotsky. You try to redistribute some of that growth to the people that need it.

Indeed such a housing system seems in direct contradiction

to the sentiment expressed in the Housing Act of 1949, not to mention the UN Declaration of Human Rights. Thus it would seem the ultimate answer to New York's housing crisis is a city that recognizes housing as an obvious right rather than a commodity.

Chapter 5

On January 19, 2017 the *New York Times* ran a story that probably caused a certain class of readers to do a double-take. It turns out that a year had gone by without there being a single shooting in the Queensbridge Houses. As for a homicide it had been almost 2 years (these streaks were unfortunately broken in May 2017 with the shooting death of a parolee. There has been another homicide in 2018). The famous, or long derided as "infamous," 96 building Queensbridge Houses is the largest public housing project in North America. The houses are famous for having a legitimate claim to being the birthplace of hip-hop, though of course the South Bronx also has its claim to that throne, and infamous for being an area that many went out of their way to avoid. Queensbridge native Nas may have opened his legendary *Illmatic* album with references to MAC-10s and stick-up kids but such things have become much less prominent in the years since. Thanks not only to security improvements but also to local community efforts, including one local group named 696 Queensbridge, crime continues to decline. Lest it be said that safety only comes from militarized tedium, 2016 featured only 11 recorded stop-and-frisks. 2015 had 15 – this in contrast to the insane 2365 stops in 2003.

Roughly a year after Queensbridge Houses reached its milestone, a frustrated City Council Speaker, Corey Johnson, implored then housing authority chairwomen Shola Olatoye to, "Just apologize...Just say, 'We are sorry that it's gotten to this point.'" Johnson was referring to the revelation that four out of five public housing residents, 323,098 in total, went without heat at some point the previous 4 months of a particularly brutal winter. The average heat outage lasted 48 hours. This was on top of 2395 heat outages in the calendar year 2017 and 4112 hot water outages (compared to 916 in 2016).[1]

Overlapping the trouble of aging, malfunctioning boilers an even worse scandal was taking shape. On November 14, 2017 the city's Investigation Department released a report describing that the housing authority knew that its inspectors were not conducting apartment inspections for lead paint in violation of federal law and that chairwoman Olatoye had falsely signed off on paperwork certifying that the inspections had been completed (Olatoye also appeared to be untruthful on the matter in testimony to the city council a month later). She went on to resign in April 2018. Analysis by the *New York Daily News* shows that from 2012 to 2016, 820 children tested positive for elevated lead levels of 5 to 9 micro-grams per deciliter of blood.[2] The city, using a higher standard of 10 micro-grams (since 2012 the Center for Disease Control has recommended intervention for infants to 5-year-olds using the 5 micro-gram standard), originally only admitted 19 children had tested for elevated blood-levels in the past decade. In response the city responded by adopting the federal standard and announcing a large plan to inspect 130,000 apartments run by the housing authority (out of 175,000). In early 2018, after a lawsuit was filed by the US attorney's office in Manhattan charging the housing authority with systematic misconduct, the housing authority entered into a settlement agreeing to a federal monitor to oversee the housing authority's compliance.

New York Housing Authority faces annual operating deficits of tens of millions of dollars along with nearly $32 billion in unmet capital needs largely due to divestment by the federal government. In other words, while public housing in New York is fulfilling its original mandate of providing safe, affordable housing it is being neglected on a local level and losing its funding on a federal level. If the city's housing projects have long been despised by the middle class as vectors of crime and disorder, and the bane of critics as far back as Jane Jacobs for their shabby modernist design, they have become a bulwark of affordable housing. Over 200,000 applicants currently sit on a waiting list. New York's public housing system is by far the largest in the US. Its 392,259 residents is a larger population than the populations of Arlington, New Orleans, and Wichita.

Various proposals to raise funds have been put forward including raising money from wealthy former residents (such as Jay-Z, Kareem Abdul-Jabbar, Howard Schultz) the way universities do, raising parking fees, and leasing the ground floors of buildings to commercial businesses. One especially controversial plan is selling underutilized land on public housing property to developers. For one thing, it is not entirely clear what would constitute underutilized land. Many of the city's public housing projects were built according to Le Corbusier's now dreaded "Tower in the park" concept. While certainly no longer in vogue, and for good reasons, it is not clear at this point that eliminating the park element is desirable. The idea was first floated by Bloomberg with de Blasio taking it up in his first term after criticizing the idea in his first mayoral campaign. De Blasio's vision is to have more of the development be for affordable apartments than Bloomberg envisioned, though as we've seen the definition of "affordable" is a fluid one. Even if this plan is enacted on a large scale it would at best mean a one-time injection of funds.

More significant is the program known as PACT (Permanent Affordability Commitment Together). PACT falls under the US Department of Housing and Urban Development (HUD) program Rental Assistance Demonstration (RAD). Created by the Obama Administration RAD shifts public housing to Section 8 housing by contracting with private developers to manage public housing units, while NYCHA (and apparently other local public housing authorities) continues to own the land and have oversight and veto power. The contracts are automatically renewed every 20 years, in theory keeping the apartments perpetually affordable. According to the PACT webpage provisions for tenants overlap with those of public housing including paying no more than 30 percent of income on rent, automatic renewal for tenants in good standing, and a right to a hearing to resolve grievances. The developer, in exchange for funding improvements and managing the property, gets the federal subsidy and presumably most, if not all, the rent payments. NYCHA has the right to retake control after a certain period.

The first project in New York under PACT was the 1,400 apartments of the Ocean Bay Houses in Queens. NYCHA partnered with RDC Development on what is listed as a $560 million rehabilitation. Since that declared success, NYCHA has identified 1,700 scattered apartments in the Bronx and Brooklyn for what it hopes will be $300 million worth of investment by 2020. Just as the public-private partnerships the city established with its parks system, undoubtedly PACT will provide physical improvements to New York's public housing. However, such arrangements raise long-term questions about the viability of public space. Private interests have a way of becoming dominant.

On November 14, 2018 a federal judge rejected the settlement that the housing authority brought to the US attorney's office. The judge, William H. Pauley, citing what he called the "breathtaking scope" of squalid living conditions in New York's public housing, strongly suggested that the federal government take over control. A settlement was reached on February 1, 2019 which avoided a complete federal takeover while replacing the authority's chairperson and installing a monitor. The city recommitted to spending $2.2 billion on repairs over the next decade. The FHA, under Ben Carson, didn't announce any funding increase – federal funding has been cut by $2.7 billion since 2001.

NYCHA goes back to 1934. It was founded in the glow of Europe's public housing expansion. From 1919 to 1933 Europe added 6 million housing units, half of them public housing. Under the London County Council over 25,000 units of council housing were built by 1932, a million by 1938. In a period known as "Red Vienna," starting in 1919 the Social Democratic city council in Vienna embarked on a radical building program of social housing, building 60,000 units in 10 years. Conservatives in the US had long opposed similar efforts, along with the real estate industry, as a threat to private property; however with the Depression raging and few new houses being built such opposition was for the time being overcome.

Of course, a critical justification in the midst of Depression was creating jobs. Public works projects have long been used by cities to absorb surplus capital in times of economic crisis. The aftermath of the crisis of 1848 saw Louis Bonaparte rise to power to become the emperor of France in 1852. A year later Bonaparte brought Haussmann to Paris to oversee public works. Haussmann, through debt-financed projects that provided working-class employment, would erect the lovely boulevards through the city and thus transform Paris into the "city of light."[3] In the wake of the financial crisis of 2008 the Chinese government embarked on a historical program of urbanization building "ghost cities" (cities without inhabitants) and tens of thousands of miles of high-speed railroads.

The first project completed by the NYCHA, indeed the first public housing in the US, was First Houses in 1934 (Atlanta's Techwood Houses were completed a year later but dedicated a year earlier). Located on the Lower East Side, First Houses turned out to be unique in New York's public housing in that it was something of a renovation project. The project consists of eight four- or five-story buildings that, while doing away with the tenements that stood before, fit within the scale of the surrounding blocks.

Next came the Williamsburg Houses, the first large-scale development followed shortly thereafter by the Harlem River Houses. These first three projects proved to be surprisingly expensive. Each were walkups leading the city to conclude that if more of the working class was to be housed the buildings would have to be taller, elevator buildings. The shift in New York and other cities in the late 1930s to "tower in the park" model was not only in line with modernist architectural theory but with economic efficiency.

From the beginning New York's public housing faced major questions beyond its architectural design. For one, there was the question of racial integration. Beyond that was the even greater question of who should live in the new public housing. This was something that even its proponents had disagreed on. There were progressive slum reformers influenced by the Great Depression and work of Elizabeth Wood that saw slum housing as a market failure necessitating slum clearance and public housing for the very poor, extending only as far as the market failure. This view was challenged by modern housing planners, centered around Catherine Bauer and her book *Modern Housing*, that wanted more public housing on vacant land, particularly in the outer parts of cities. Bauer was impressed by the large-scale work of Bauhaus architects on the outskirts of German cities, that would target the working class (i.e. not the poorest citizens).[4] According to Nicholas Bloom in *Public Housing that Worked*, the NYCHA took a more politically realistic, perhaps conservative, approach than did cities such as Chicago and St Louis. Rather than see public housing as an instrument for integration, in its early days the NYCHA was careful that the inhabitants of public housing largely reflected their surrounding neighborhoods. This meant that in 1941 zero black families lived in First Houses, one black family lived in the Williamsburg Houses (along with 1621 white families), 52 lived in Queensbridge (3097 white families), and Harlem River Houses were completely made up of black families. While this approach certainly reinforced a segregated status quo it did have the effect of softening any resistance in white neighborhoods therefore allowing more housing to be built in the long run, as well as maintaining a degree of integration for over a decade by keeping a white population in public housing longer than in Chicago.[5] The same kind of policy was used to tenant selection in general. New York, along with other cities early on, had a thorough tenant selection process that avoided the more idealistic vision of public housing as housing for the poorest of the poor. NYCHA's approach, which soon had to maneuver through Federal regulations, used a point system that emphasized factors including employment history, salary, and marital status. In 1968 the federal Department of HUD required local housing authorities to use a first come-first served system for tenant application officially eliminating the ability to use screening in tenant selection. New York battled federal regulations keeping its screening regulations longer than other cities (For instance, by 1940 Chicago's housing authority was targeting the poorest families).

It is difficult in the present age of privatization and wealth driven nostalgia for restored factories and brownstones to conceive the ethos that drove the movement for public housing. No less a figure than Eleanor Roosevelt was present at the opening of First Houses. FDR himself attended the dedication of Atlanta's Techwood Houses where he proclaimed "Here, at the request of the citizens of Atlanta, we have cleaned out nine blocks of antiquated squalid dwellings, for years a detriment to this community. Today those hopeless old houses are gone and in their place we see the bright cheerful buildings of the Techwood Housing Project." New York's most iconic mayor, Fiorello LaGuardia, thundered in 1944, his last year in office, "Tear down the old. Build up the new. Down with rotten, antiquated rat holes. Down with hovels. Down with disease. Down with crime. Down with firecraft. Let in the sun. Let in the sky. A new day is dawning. A new life. A new America!"

The rhetoric matches the ethic of modernism, described by Owen Hatherley in his book *Militant Modernism* as "not merely progress but an interruption, a rapture, a break with the continuum altogether, regardless of how much it would be settled back into it later."[6] Nathan Glazer described modernism like so: "Modernism was a movement, with much larger intentions than replacing the decorated tops of buildings with flat roofs, molded window frames with flat trips of metal, curves and curlicues with straight lines. It represented a rebellion against historicism, ornament, overblown form, pandering to the great and rich and newly rich as against serving the needs of a society's common people."[7] Architectural modernism is often summarized by the oft repeated aphorisms "Less is More," popularized by Mies van der Rohe, and "Form follows function," first coined by less famous earlier American architect Lewis Sullivan. It meant simply that the purpose of the building should be the starting point for its design (the original quote was "Form ever follows function"). Characterized by such details as asymmetrical compositions, flat roofs, concrete bases, and an absence of ornament or decoration, modernism saw itself as more than a school of architecture. It was a movement about a pure use of materials and building a better world. While there are plenty of office buildings that were built along modernist lines the vision of its pioneers was housing for the masses.

The federal Housing Act of 1937, also known as the Wagner-Steagall Act, established the United States Housing Authority (today HUD) in order to "provide assistance to state and local governments for the elimination of unsafe and unsanitary conditions, for the eradication of slums, for the provision of decent, safe, and sanitary dwellings for families of low income, and for the reduction of unemployment and the stimulation of business activity..."

While conservative opposition took a backseat in the very creation of public housing it was by no means muted nor was its effect on how public housing developed. There were limits placed on construction costs. The bill authorized only $5000 per unit. The earliest public housing projects were for the most part the most architecturally interesting: however the cost containment led to short cuts, inferior materials, and limited design; in some buildings elevators stopped on every other floor, cement floors were installed along with cinder block walls. This was especially the case when the US Housing Authority pressured local authorities to reduce costs even beyond the skimpy federal guidelines in a misguided attempt to persuade public housing opponents that the program could be cost effective.[8]

Cost controls would remain a critical factor. As post-World War II suburbanization took off, again helped greatly by government largess in highway building and FHA mortgages, and advances were made regarding building materials and efficiency, along with plenty of open space, building private housing in Levittowns became cheaper than clearing away slums to build public housing (the suburbs obviously took a large chunk of the white working class as well). This increased the burden to justify costs putting further pressure on public housing designs.

Local housing authorities were required to partner with local governments to build any housing and there was an "equivalent elimination" clause that required for every unit of public housing built one unit of substandard housing would have to be taken down. This meant that local politics would dictate where public housing was built which meant that the bulk of public housing would be built in poorer neighborhoods and would enforce racial segregation (local real estate interests were able to whip up hysteria about public housing being a threat to segregation). This was obviously true in southern states but not exclusively; Chicago saw white mob violence initially have a big impact on public housing placement. Certainly it was poor neighborhoods, particularly black neighborhoods, that needed a massive upgrade in housing conditions; progressive reformers for decades pushed for slum clearance on the basis that poor living conditions not only spread disease but fostered delinquency and disorder as well, yet building more public housing on vacant land or in desirable locations would have reduced segregation to the present day along with the stigmatization with which public housing would soon be labeled.

The main point of these legislative features was to ensure public housing wouldn't directly compete with the private housing market. Senator Wagner, who co-sponsored the bill, would say at the time "the most important consideration is, that public housing projects should not be brought into competition with private industry...To reach those who are really entitled to public assistance, and to get into the field where private enterprise cannot operate, is the objective of this bill" (in New York this extended to commercial interests as well. If the current idea is to place stores in public housing, the early impetus was eliminating them). Given that the very point of public enterprise should be to compete with and restrain the excess of private interests and provide a viable public option, to the extent public housing was prevented from doing this it was set up to be at least marginalized from the start – "Housing of the last resort" was destined to have a hard road.

Within 2 decades cracks were appearing. Being the dominant school of architecture, modernism, and by extension the public housing that theoretically was built according to its precepts, drew its prominent critics. Most famously Jane Jacobs in *The Life and Death of American Cities* (1961) castigated public housing tower blocks for their banality and isolation. If the original purpose was to insulate public housing from the slums that often surrounded it, Jacobs saw the disruption of neighborhood networks. In 1966 Robert Venturi published his Complexity and Contradiction in Architecture. Turning Mies van der Rohe's "Less is more" maxim on its head, proclaiming "Less is a bore," Venturi said of modern architects: "In their attempt to break with tradition and start all over again, they idealized the primitive and elementary at the expense of the diverse and the sophisticated. As participants in a revolutionary movement, they acclaimed the newness of modern functions, ignoring their contradictions."[9]

Some years later in 1981 Tom Wolfe jumped into the fray with From Bauhaus to Our House. Lamenting the nonappearance of a "totally new American architecture" and the large influence of European modernism, he wrote: "the reigning architectural style in this, the very Babylon of capitalism, became worker housing," adding cynically and wrongly: "But somehow the workers, intellectually undeveloped as they were, managed to avoid public housing. The workers – if by workers we mean people who have jobs – headed out to the suburbs."[10] For what it's worth, Wolfe was equally unimpressed about Venturi, claiming Venturi simply "brought Modernism into its Scholastic Age."

The modernist era is said, first by Charles Jenaks in The Language of Post-Modern Architecture, to have come to an end with the dynamiting of the Pruitt-Igoe public housing development in St Louis. Jenaks: "Modern Architecture died in St. Louis, Missouri on July 15, 1972 at 3:32pm (or thereabouts) when the infamous Pruitt-Igoe scheme, or rather several of its slab blocks, were given the final coup de grace by dynamite.[11]" Pruitt-Igoe, designed by Minouri Yamasaki, most famous for designing the original World Trade Center, was especially poorly run public housing. It opened in 1954 but residents rejected the complex almost immediately. Before 5 years went by the project was 16 percent vacant. Before it was 15 years old Pruitt-Igoe was two-thirds empty.[12] A year later Nixon declared a *moratorium on housing and community development assistance* and 2 years later Congress passed the Housing and Community Development Act of 1974 establishing the Section 8 program where the government provides vouchers for low-income tenants to rent from private landlords willing to participate in the program. By 2000 Section 8, later renamed the Housing Choice Voucher Program, surpassed public housing as the largest housing assistance program in the country.

Like all such bold declarations, this is quite overstated. Even at its peak, high-rises only represented 27 percent of public housing, and these were concentrated in several large cities. This fact didn't stop high-rises from dominating the perception and coverage of public housing. The open, green space that was supposed to provide a clean, open environment was deemed a space for violence and gang wars. The protection from the surrounding slums the tower block model was supposed to provide took away what Jane Jacobs called "the eyes of the street." In 1972, shortly before Pruitt-Igoe was slated for destruction, Oscar Newman published his influential study Defensible Space: Crime Prevention through Urban Design that compared two neighboring public housing projects in Brooklyn, one made up of 14-story buildings (the Van Dyke Houses), the other a mix of three- and six-story walkups (the Brownsville Houses). Predictably Newman found that to some extent vandalism and crime were issues in both projects but were less so in the walkups due to what he termed "defensible space."

This too was exaggerated. The relationship between crime and public housing is complex. High-rise living is not considered a problem for the rich. Consider Jefferson's theme song of "moving on up" to a "deluxe apartment in the sky." The newest tallest buildings in New York are apartment buildings for the very wealthy that are exponentially taller than any public housing. In New York, where up until 1995 the city's housing authority had its own police and thereby kept reliable statistics, public housing was on average 60 percent safer than the city at large through the mid-1970s. In 1967 public housing complexes were 42 percent safer than New York's streets, by 1974 they were 78 percent safer. This would be reversed during the crack epidemic of the late 1980s.[13]

Bradford Hunt makes the convincing argument that many of the problems that the Chicago Housing Authority, probably the worst run housing authority in the country, experienced had their roots in harsh demographics – namely the ratio of youths to adults. A typical Chicago neighborhood in 1960 had slightly more than one youth (defined as aged 25 and younger) for every two adults, a youth density of 0.58. By 1965 the CHA's overall youth density was 2.11, over two youths for every adult, basically inverting the city average. The Robert Taylor Houses opened in Chicago in 1963 with a youth density of 2.86. In no similar sized community had there been so many youths supervised by so few adults.[14] The Pruitt-Igoe complex had a similar youth density of 2.63 in 1968.[15] This was a matter of poor, if understandable, planning. Public Housing in Chicago was geared toward families with children for good reasons. However, planners were unable to adjust for reasons both of competence and politics. This history serves to illustrate the complexity. It shows there is nothing inherent regarding crime and public housing.

Complexity aside it is safe to say that by the mid-1970s the idea of public housing was synonymous with crime, disorder, and cultural barbarism. Yet the thing is cities themselves were also thought of in such terms. To that extent public housing simply was an extension of the American city. Chicago's public housing was the most notorious in the country (spotlighted by Alex Kotlowitz's 1992 *There are No Children Here)*. Yet even with a large amount of its public housing gone, Chicago's Southside is to this day held up as a symbol of urban chaos. In fact, in the case of Chicago it has been theorized that the displacement of residents from public housing to neighborhoods already under strained resources, particularly after the foreclosure crisis that began in 2007-08, has been a cause of continuing crime.[16] In that sense the question of well-run public housing in the midst of urban crisis misses the forest from the trees. In a period of capital flight, loss of industrial jobs, and the withdrawal of the state all severely impacting cities, how much could have been expected of public housing? Have not gallons of sympathetic ink now been spilled on such factors and their effect on the mythicized white working class and the Trump presidency? If it was the fate of the majority of public housing, due to a convergence of factors progressive and reactionary, to be built as a result of slum clearance, and if the dynamics that created the slums in the first place certainly were not alleviated, in fact they accelerated, than how could public housing not to some extent reflect that reality? As poverty and crime went up along with public assistance rolls increasing through the 1960s, the working-class family was decimated as single parenthood skyrocketed; could public housing, set up as housing as the last resort from the beginning, not be impacted?

Still despite all that, a congressional commission was formed in 1989; the National Commission of Severely Distressed Public Housing was formed to investigate the matter of distressed public housing. It found that only 6 percent of units nationwide were severely distressed. This total of 6 percent wasn't completely insignificant (amounting to roughly 86,000 units) but neither was it a national crisis. The commission's report, released in 1992, read: "It is important to note that if 6% of the units are severely distressed, approximately 94% of the units are not in such a state; thus, the public housing program continues to provide an important rental housing resource for many low-income families and others."

Acknowledging the obvious problems, 80 percent of public housing residents lived below the poverty threshold, the commission's recommendations included an emphasis on rehabilitation of units wherever possible and the replacement of any units which needed to be demolished, and replacement units to be in the same neighborhoods as the removed ones. Other recommendations included experimenting with alternative management structures (nonprofits, private management companies, resident managed, etc.).

What came out of the report was the HOPE VI program. The point of the HOPE VI program was to provide federal grants to replace distressed public housing with mixed-income communities. The commission's report found 86,000 distressed units and recommended rehabilitation. Since HOPE VI was passed about 250,000 units have been demolished with only around 50,000 replaced – meaning obviously that the HOPE VI program has gone far beyond the commission's recommendations.

While public housing has long been stigmatized as crime-ridden hellholes it is notable that the epoch of demolition is taking place at a time of plummeting urban crime rates, and that the drop in crime preceded the large majority of the demolition. What changed in the early 1990s was the context. The GOP takeover of Congress in 1994, including winning the House of Representatives for the first time since 1954, with the requisite threats to abolish HUD altogether was a factor but probably not the most prominent one. Most prominent was that, given the see-saw nature of capital, and the inevitable rent-gaps growing, capital began to flow back into cities it had once fled from making many central cities neighborhoods ripe for gentrification. A barrier to increased private investment was some challenged public housing. The Techwood Housing Project in Atlanta was demolished (with the exception of a few buildings preserved for historic landmarks) in preparation for Atlanta's hosting of the 1996 Olympics. The redone complex, converting 1195 units of public housing into 800 units of mixed housing, was rechristened Centennial Place. The infamous Cabrini-Green Housing in Chicago was located on the city's prosperous Near North Side and was torn down as part of the city's Plan for Transformation. Residential property sales in the two-block radius around Cabrini-Green totaled less than $6 million in 1995. Five years later, at the start of the Plan for Transformation, annual sales were $120 million, and from 2000 to 2005, total sales reached $1 billion.[17] Allen Parkway Village, in Houston's gentrifying Fourth Ward, adjacent to the downtown area, became the Historic Oaks of Allen Parkway Village.

By 2011 Atlanta had demolished all of its public housing. Chicago demolished the most in sheer numbers but many other cities, including Las Vegas, Baltimore, Harford, Memphis, and Pittsburgh tore down at least some of their stock. The stated policy justification for the shift was the elimination of concentrated poverty through the development of mixed neighborhoods. New Urbanism, with its emphasis on walkability and connectivity, was solidifying itself as the dominant form of design ensuring that architectural integration and access to the streets would define the new mixed-income developments.

There is an obvious inherent democratic quality to the idea of mixed-income neighborhoods. Economic diversity would seem to imply a kind of equality of access, less polarization, and perhaps even more compassionate neighbors. Middle-class and above residents are considered, by obvious virtue of their wealth, to be more effective neighborhood advocates, their buying power a stimulus for local businesses. The problem with these new mixed-income developments is that they were created by displacement, indeed displacement was the very point. Estimates are that only 14 to 25 percent of the original residents return to the redeveloped sites[18]. Most of the displaced move on average about 3 miles away from their original homes to neighborhoods perhaps marginally less poor and segregated than the neighborhood they are displaced from, but still poorer than the city average, and certainly still more segregated[19]. It is ironic that a major criticism of public housing was that local neighborhoods were bulldozed and inhabitants removed to build it, while a generation later it is public housing residents being displaced to rebuild modern, and much richer, versions of the neighborhoods that were earlier cleared.

This leads to a deeper issue, namely its one-sided nature. It would be difficult to argue against a policy that somehow guaranteed all neighborhoods of a city were mixed-income neighborhoods – in other words requiring an average level of poverty and low-income housing in the wealthiest neighborhoods (say the Upper East Side and Brooklyn Heights in New York). Instead the vast majority of mixed-income development is accomplished through the deliberate gentrification of poor and working-class neighborhoods. Politics forbids the former and actively promotes the latter. One program that attempted to allow, and study, the effects of moving poorer families into wealthier neighborhoods was the Move to Opportunity program. A total of 4608 families enrolled in the program of which 1700 randomly selected participants moved out of high poverty neighborhoods to low poverty ones (two other groups were formed to compare with that group: a control group which received no vouchers but remained eligible for public housing and a traditional voucher group which received regular Section 8 vouchers). The study lasted for years with much analyzed results but as to the ideal of wealthier neighborhoods becoming more economically diverse, the program ran into immediate white backlash in Congress and was capped, thereby blocked from any national-level expansion.

The results of Move to Opportunity and HOPE VI mirror each other. Some studies report residents feel a loss of community and social ties of public housing.[20] Residents in general report feeling safer in their new environments. Important as a greater sense of safety is for physical and mental health, one could say that is the very point of a home, an area where there is little to no evidence for improvement is residents' economic well-being (in the Move to Opportunity program some studies show the arrest rate of young men moving to wealthier areas actually increased[21]) . Here building mixed-income developments seems to fall into the same environmental determinism that drove earlier public housing. If modernist architects believed the environments they were building would not only improve housing conditions of slum dwellers but also their entire being, the same is just as untrue for mixed-income replacements, indeed with gentrification in general (it's no coincidence that Andres

Duany, founder of the Congress for New Urbanism, penned a screed called "Three Cheers for Gentrification"). The vision of poor people absorbing the alleged glorious industrious values of their wealthier neighbors rings as true as the mythology that measured the amount of light needed to cure poverty. Lance Freeman writing in *There Goes the 'Hood: Views of Gentrification From The Ground Up* probably comes the closest to the dynamic when he suggests:

> For the most part, the residents who had lived in the neighborhood for a while, who would not be considered gentrifiers, typically described the gentry as a people who are not interwoven into the social fabric of the community. The two groups were sharing residential space and cordial, but it seems unlikely that the indigenous residents of the neighborhood would find themselves mimicking the behavior of their more affluent neighbors as the peer effects model would imply.[22]

What this proves is, as vital as housing is to a good life, it must been symbiotic with an economy that provides the working class with secure employment and a true living wage.

Much recent ink has been spilled lamenting Americans' new lack of mobility. According to the Census Bureau about 10 percent of Americans moved in 2017, down from the 1950s through the early 1980s when more than 20 percent of the population moved. Tyler Cohen, in his book *The Complacent Class: The Self-Defeating Quest for the American Dream*, laments that the interstate migration rate has fallen 51 percent below the average rate from 1948-71. Yet the big cities that are meant to be drawing workers from the country's stagnant regions are the same cities with massive homeless populations. New York has a homeless population of over 63,000. The Bay Area, DC, Seattle and others have seen homelessness explode in recent years. In the last 7 years the homeless population of Los Angeles has surged by 75 percent.[23]

New housing construction has been heavily concentrated in the luxury markets of these major cities. In 2016, 40 percent of construction went for rentals of $1500 and higher; a further 25 percent for rentals $1100-1499.[24] Greater density is greener and an incubator for innovation so more building is welcome; however, as a People's Policy Project report "Social Housing in the United States" points out, deregulation and increased supply is no cure-all for the current housing crisis of cities. Even if new buildings would trickle down to lower incomes as they age it would take decades. The federal Low-Income Housing Tax Credit, a tax credit for developers for building low-income housing, is far too small. Inclusive Zoning, setting aside a set number of apartments for lower incomes, isn't causing much of a dent. There is still a need for public housing.

For its loud failures in the US we still have plenty of examples of successful public housing. New York's crime rate is at an all-time low and the city has barely touched its public housing. Boston redeveloped its Commonwealth Development, replacing a distressed housing project with a well-designed community rehousing most of the project's older residents.[25] Globally there is the gold standard of Vienna where 62 percent of the city's population lives in subsidized housing, 20 percent is run by the city, the rest by nonprofits. Vienna's social housing is both architecturally innovative and well managed. More such housing is in the pipeline – about one-third of new housing is social housing. Barcelona features the gorgeously hip Torre Placa Europa. Council housing in Britain, despite large-scale privatization since the Thatcher years, still houses 8 percent of people.

And why could it not be mixed? Vienna's social housing is available for anyone earning up to $53,225 after taxes (the country's median income is about $31,500, meaning about 80 percent of the population is eligible). Including higher-income residents, still at lower rents than the private sector, would both bring money and avoid concentrated poverty. It was boxing public housing into housing of the last resort that was at the root of many of its problems. Featuring things like architectural design contests these new projects could be built into true local competition to the speculative private real estate market. The People's Policy Project report recommends 10 million new municipal units over 10 years as a viable goal.

Public housing solutions face strong obstacles and would need activism toward every level of government. In 1997 the state legislature stripped the city council's authority to repeal the vacancy decontrol. The 1971 Urstadt Law prohibits the city from putting in place further local rent laws without the approval of Albany, making the battle an uphill one (the city can weaken renter protections but not add to them). The law could be overturned and rent laws returned to city governance.

As for architecture, for modernism's failures real and perceived, Nathan Glazer wrote in a 2007 essay titled "What Happened to the Social Agenda" of architects:

> The architect could then conclude that if modernism could do nothing for social problems, if the expectations of architectural determinism were naïve, why bother: Let us devote ourselves to architecture alone – to building design and form – instead of to architecture and city planning.[26]

In other words, status quo, political neutral buildings that reflect the excess of the global elite while demonstrating no purpose beyond their own genius. New York will never run out of such works. Walk up Broadway from City Hall and one will catch sight of Frank Gehry's very chic 8 Spruce St, with an average rent of $5500 a month. Meanwhile over on the Lower East Side, the corner of Delancey and Essex streets display a close-up view of Bernard Tschumi's Blue Condominium. The average sale price there is $1.5 million. Cutting through Chelsea is the much lauded Highline, a 1.45-mile elevated park built on the leftover tracks from New York Central Railroad's West Side Freight Line. Opened in 2009 the Highline draws raves from planners worldwide along with millions of visitors a year. It was soon surrounded by a stream of starchitect designs including Gehry's IAC Building (completed in 2007) and Norman Foster's 551 21st Street, and the late Zara Hadid. Hadid, renowned for being the first female recipient of the Pritzker Prize, also became somewhat infamous for an August 2014 answer to an interview question about the brutal working conditions in Dubai where she designed the Al Wakrah stadium for the 2022 World Cup. When questioned about the fatal conditions for construction workers Hadid coldly replied: "I have nothing to do with the workers. I think that's an issue the government – if there's a problem – should pick up. Hopefully, these things will be resolved." While there have been no worker fatalities building 520 West 28th, the social effect for New York can be inferred from the prices that range from just under $5 million up to $50 million per unit.

Cross Fifth Avenue and find Rem Koulhass' glass-covered 121 East 22nd Street. A little further uptown on First Avenue stands the American Cooper Buildings. Designed by SHoP Architects, these twin towers feature a copper facade with a three-story sky bridge connecting them – the bridge is equipped with a gym and 75-foot lap pool (SHoP also designed the hideous Barclays Center in Brooklyn for the Nets).

It goes without saying that architects can't determine city planning policy on their own, yet there is no reason, given the housing crisis ravaging many cities, for the profession not to push the envelope in a more inclusive direction. And there is no inherent reason such a movement would have to return to the bland bricks of modernism's housing projects. Earlier 2016 Pritzker Prize winner, Chilean architect Alejandro Aravena, posted a number of his designs for low-cost housing for free on his firm Elemental's webpage. In an interview with Dezeen, Aravena said of architects and social housing: "But the constraints are not just budget constraints – the building logic, the political framework, and the policies, are part of the equation and we're not well trained for that. We're never taught the right thing at university."

One can only hope that changes. Architects can be valuable allies to progressive city planning. It wasn't all that long ago that architecture represented something besides extreme global inequality and cultural homogeneity. For that to happen, though, the word "starchitect" would have to take on a different, and grander, meaning.

Endnotes

Chapter 1

1   Jose A Del Real, "The Bronx's Quiet, Brutal War with Opioids," New York Times, October 12, 2017

2   https://www.rentcafe.com/blog/rental-market/real-estate-news/top-20-neighborhoods-with-most-apartments-post-recession/

3   Emily Badger, "The Same Cities keep attracting Tech. Why?" New York Times, November 5, 2018

4   https://eig.org/dynamism

5   The Citizens Budget Commission, "10 Billion Reasons to Rethink Economic Development in New York," February 11, 2019

6   Cited in Joshua B. Freeman, Working Class New York: Life and Labor Since World War II (The New Press, New York, 2000), 8

7   Freeman, Working Class New York, 11

8   Melissa Loomis Bindra "The Politics and Policies of New York City's Manufacturing Industry," PhD Diss, Columbia University, May 2017

9   Marc Levinson, The Box: How the Shipping Container Made the World Smaller and the World Economy Bigger (Princeton University Press, New Jersey, 2016), 105

10 Aaron Shkuda, "The Downtown Lower Manhattan Association," PhD diss., University of Chicago, 2009

11 Freeman, Working Class New York, 163

12 Levinson, 112

13 Vincent Cannato, The Ungovernable City: John Lindsay and his Struggle to Save New York (Basic Books, New York, 2001), 106-7

14 Quoted from ed. Loretta Lees, Tom Slater, and Elvin Wyly, The Gentrification Reader (Routledge: New York, 2010), 7

15 Loretta Lees, Tom Slater, and Elvin Wyly, Gentrification (Routledge: New York, 2008), 5

16 Suleiman Osman, The Invention of Brownstone Brooklyn: Gentrification and the Search for Authenticity in Postwar New York (Oxford University Press, New York, 2011), 27

17 Osman, The Invention of Brownstone Brooklyn, 87

18 Lees, Slater, Wyly, Gentrification, 27

19 Kay S. Hymowitz, The New Brooklyn: What it Takes to Bring a City Back (Rowman & Littlefield, Maryland, 2017), 44

20 Andrew Cherlin, Labor's Lost Love: The Rise and Fall of the Working Class Family (Russell Sage Foundation, New York, 2014)

21 Osman, The Invention of Brownstone Brooklyn, 88

22 Lee, Slater, Wyly, Gentrification, 28; calculated from data from Tom O'Hanlon, "Neighborhood Change in New York City: A Case Study of Park Slope 1850 through 1980," PhD diss, City University of New York, 1982 (available online)

23 Neil Smith, "Toward a Theory of Gentrification: A Back to the City Movement by Capital, Not People," Journal of the American Planning Association 45 (4): 538–48

24 David Harvey, "From Managerialism to Entrepreneurialism: The Transformation in Urban Governance in Late Capitalism," Geografiska Annaler. Series B, Human Geography, Vol. 71, No. 1, The Roots of Geographical Change: 1973 to the Present (1989), pp. 3-17

25 Saskia Sassen, The Global City, (Princeton University Press, New Jersey, 2001), 40

26 Smith, Neil, "New Globalism, New Urbanism: Gentrification as Global Urban Strategy," Antipode 34 (2002): 434–57

27 Lee, Slater, Wyly, Gentrification, 181

28 Saskia Sassen, "Who owns our cities – and why this urban takeover should concern us all," The Guardian, November 24, 2015

29 Jamie Peck, "Liberating the City: Between New York and

New Orleans," *Urban Geography*, 27 (2006): 681-713

30 Aaron Shkuda, The Lofts of SoHo: Gentrification, Art, and Industry in New York, 1950-1980, (The University of Chicago Press: Chicago, 2016), 15

31 Shkuda, The Lofts of SoHo, 27

32 Sharon Zukin, Loft Living: Culture and Capital in Urban Change, (Johns Hopkins University Press: Baltimore, 1982), 39

33 Zukin, Loft Living, 40

34 Zukin, Loft Living, 33

35 Carl Grodach, Nichole Foster, James Murdoch "Gentrification, displacement, and the arts: Untangling the relationship between arts industries and place change," Urban Studies, Vol 55, Issue 4, December 6, 2016

36 Shkuda, The Lofts of SoHo, 89-90

37 Quoted in Winifred Curran, "Gentrification and the Nature of Work: exploring the links in Williamsburg Brooklyn," Environment and Planning A 2004, Volume 36 ,1250

38 Curran, 1250

39 Tom Angotti "Zoning Instead of Planning in Greenpoint and Williamsburg," Gotham Gazette, May 17, 2005

40 Carl Campanile "These are the biggest losers in Brooklyn's gentrification," New York Post, November 6, 2017

41 Martin Gottlieb "FHA CASE RECALLS BUSHWICK IN 70'S," New York Times, February 2, 1986

42 Jonathan Mahler, Ladies and Gentlemen, The Bronx is Burning: 1977, Baseball, Politics, and The Battle for The Soul Of a City, (Farrar, Straus and Giroux: New York, 2005), 211

43 Mahler, Ladies and Gentlemen, The Bronx is Burning, 197

44 John A. Dereszewski, "Bushwick Notes: From the 70's to Today" (available online)

45 Lee Dembart "Carter Takes 'Sobering,'" New York Times, October 6 1977

46 Roger Starr "Making New York Smaller," New York Times,

November 14, 1976

47 Francis X. Clines "Blighted Areas' Use Is Urged by Rohatyn," New York Times, March 16, 1976

48 Joe Flood, The Fires: How a computer formula, Big Ideas, and The Best Intentions Burned Down New York City – And Determined the Future of Cities, (Riverhead Books: New York, 2010), 170

49 Deborah and Roderick Wallace, A Plague on Your Houses: How New York was Burned Down and National Public Health Crumbled, (Verso, London, 1998)

50 Flood, The Fires, 246

51 Flood, The Fires, 18

52 Jonathan Soffer, Ed Koch and the Rebuilding of New York City, (Columbia University Press, New York, 2012), 303

53 Dereszewski, Bushwick Notes

54 Philip Ball, "Gentrification is a natural evolution," The Guardian, November 19, 2014

55 Kay Hymowitz, The New Brooklyn: What it Takes to Bring a City Back, (Rowman & Littlefield Publishers, New York, 2017), 165

56 Hymowitz, The New Brooklyn, 50

57 Lance Freeman and Frank Braconi "Gentrification and displacement: New York City in the 1990s," Journal of the American Planning Association, 70 (1), 39-52

58 Katie Newman and Elvin K. Wyly "The Right to Stay Put, Revisited: Gentrification and Resistance to Displacement in New York City," Urban Studies, vol. 43, issue 1, January 2006, 23-57

59 Peter Marcuse, "Gentrification, Abandonment, and Displacement: Connections, Causes, and Policy Response in New York City," Journal of Urban and Contemporary Law, 195, 1985

60 Rosalyn Baxandall and Elizabeth Ewan, Picture Windows: How the Suburbs Happened, (Basic Books, New York, 2000),

106-7

61 Alan Ehrenhalt, The Great Inversion and the Future of American Cities, (Alfred A. Knopf, New York, 2012)

62 Neil Smith and Michelle LeFaivre "A Class Analysis of Gentrification" (published in Gentrification, Displacement and Neighborhood Revitalization, State University of New York Press, 1984, ed. J. John Palen and Bruce London)

63 Tom Slater, "There is Nothing Natural about Gentrification," New Left Project, December 20, 2014

64 Andy Merrifield, "Fifty Years On: The Right to the City" (published in The Right to The City, ed. Verso Books)

Chapter 2

1 Lynne A. Weikart, Follow the Money: Who Controls New York City Mayors? (State University of New York Press, Albany, 2009), 110

2 Ken Auletta, The Streets Were Paved with Gold (Random House, New York, 1975), 193

3 Charles R. Morris, The Cost of Good Intentions: New York City and the Liberal Experiment (W.W. Norton & Company, New York), 185

4 Kim Moody, From Welfare State to Real Estate: Regime Change in New York City, 1974 to the Present (The New Press, New York, 2007), 52-3

5 Weikart, 34

6 Richard Pluntz, A History of Housing in New York City (Columbia University Press, New York, 1990), 281

7 Roger Starr, The Rise and Fall of New York City (Basic Books, New York, 1985)

8 Robert Fitch, The Assassination of New York (Verso, New York, 1993), ix

9 Moody, 59

10 Weikart, 34

11 Yanek Mieczkowski, Gerald Ford and the Challenges of the

1970s (University Press of Kentucky, 2005), 54

12 Mike Davis, Planet of Slums (Verso, New York, 2006)

Chapter 3

1 Max Page, The City's End: Two Centuries of Fantasies, Fears, and Premonitions of New York's Destruction, (Yale University Press, New Haven, 2008)

2 Miriam Greenberg, Branding New York: How a City in Crisis Was Sold to The World (New York: Routledge, 2008), 49

3 Lizbeth Cohen and Brian Goldsmith, Governing at the Tipping Point: Shaping the City's Role in Economic Development, in ed. by Joseph P. Viteritti, Summer in the City: John Lindsay, New York, and the American Dream, (Johns Hopkins Press, Baltimore, 2014)

4 Greenberg, Branding New York, 100

5 Greenberg, Branding New York, 223

6 The Suburbanization of New York, ed. Jerilou Hammet, Kingsley Hammet (New Jersey: Princeton Architectural Press, 2007), 19

7 Alex S. Vitale, City of Disorder: How the Quality of Life Campaign Transformed New York Politics (New York: New York University Press, 2008), 109

8 Vitale, City of Disorder, 110

9 Susan S. Fainstein, The City Builders: Property Development in New York and London, 1980-2000, 2nd Ed (Lawrence: University of Kansas Press, 2001), 38

10 Vitale, City of Disorder, 105

11 Sharon Zukin, Naked City: The Death and Life of Authentic Urban Places (New York: Oxford University Press, 2010), 144

12 Kevin Baker, Death of a Once Great City, Harper's Magazine, July 2018

13 Laura Bult, Dareh Gregorian, Sarah Ryley, "Daily News

analysis finds racial disparities in summons for minor violations in 'broken windows' policing," New York Daily News, August 4 2014

14 Benjamin Mueller, Robert Gebeloff, Sahil Chinoy, "Surest Way to Face Marijuana Charges in New York: Be Black or Hispanic," New York Times, May 13, 2018

15 https://www.nyclu.org/en/stop-and-frisk-data

16 Alice Speri, "New York Gang Database Expanded by 70 Percent Under Mayor Bill de Blasio," The Intercept, June 11, 2018

17 Zukin, Naked City, 80

18 Mike Owen Benediktsson, Brian Lamberta, and Erika Larsen, "The Real Small Business Killer," New York Daily News, October 12, 2014

19 Derek Thompson, How Manhattan Became a Rich Ghost Town, The Atlantic, October 15, 2018

20 Glenn Blain "Court Ruling Restores Limits on NYC Porn Shops," New York Daily News, June 6, 2017

21 Lynne B. Sagalyn, Times Square Roulette: Remaking the City Icon (Cambridge: MIT Press, 2001), 19

22 http://vanishingnewyork.blogspot.com/2016/08/zombie-urbanism.html

23 Christopher Mele, Selling the Lower East Side: Culture, Real Estate, and Resistance in New York City (Minneapolis: University of Virginia Press, 2000), 3

24 Office of New York State Controller Report http://www.osc.state.ny.us/osdc/hotel_industry_nyc_rpt2_2017.pdf

25 Patrick McGeehan, "NYC Is on Pace to Draw a Record 67 Million Tourists This Year," New York Times, Aug 19, 2019

26 Andrew Van Dam, "Hawaii has record-low unemployment and it's not a frozen hellscape. Why are people leaving?" Washington Post, January 5, 2018

27 Sarah Maslin Nir, "Tax Break Could Help Small Shops Survive Manhattan's Rising Rents," New York Times,

November 28, 2017

28 https://nycfuture.org/research/state-of-the-chains-2018

Chapter 4

1 Louise Story and Stephanie Saul, "Towers of Secrecy: Stream of Foreign Wealth Flows to Elite New York Real Estate," New York Times, February 7, 2015

2 https://www.icij.org/investigations/offshore/americas-island-haven-manhattan/

3 Andrew Rice, "Stash Pad: The New York real-estate market is now the premier destination for wealthy foreigners with rubles, yuan, and dollars to hide," *New York Magazine*, January 27, 2014

4 Kristen Capps, Why Billionaires Don't Pay Taxes in New York, *Citylab*, May 11, 2015

5 http://metrocosm.com/nyc-property-tax-billionaires/

6 Josh Barbanel, Why New York Values Ken Griffin's $238 Million Condo at Less Than $10 Million, *The Wall Street Journal*, February 27, 2019

7 Cezary Podkul, Thousands of NYC Landlords Who Ignored Rent Caps Got Tax Breaks They Didn't Qualify For, *ProPublica*, October 20, 2016

8 Judith Evans, "High-Rise, High-spec, High-risk," Financial Times, June 29/June 30 2019

9 Michelle Higgins, "In New York, a Falling Market for Trophy Homes in the Sky," New York Times, July 11, 2016

10 Melissa Lawford, Midtown Millennials, *Financial Times*, November 17/November 18 2018

11 Michael Gold, "As Market Cools, Median Price for Manhattan Apartment Drops Below $1million (to $999,999)," New York Times, January 3, 2019

12 Hana R. Alberts, Shocker: Half of Midtown's Super Luxury Condos Sit Vacant, *Curbed New York*, October 24, 2014

13 https://comptroller.nyc.gov/wp-content/uploads/

documents/Hidden_Households.pdf

14 http://furmancenter.org/files/sotc/Part_1_Gentrification_
    SOCin2015_9JUNE2016.pdf

15 Zoned Out: Race, Displacement, and City Planning in New
    York City, Ed by Tom Angotti and Sylvia Morse (Terreform,
    Inc., New York, 2016)

16 Walter Thabit, How East New York Became a Ghetto, (New
    York University Press, New York, 2003), 1

17 Andrew Rice, "The Red Hot Rubble of East New York," New
    York Magazine, January 28, 2015

18 Michael Greenberg, Tenants Under Siege Inside New York
    City's Housing Crisis, *New York Review of Books*, August 17,
    2017

19 https://www.dropbox.com/s/y5l9089k9c7o4nj/Banking_on_
    Vacancy%283%29.pdf?dl=0

Chapter 5

1   William Neuman, "As 4 of 5 in Public Housing Lost Heat, a
    Demand for an Apology Is Unfulfilled," New York Times,
    February 6, 2018

2   Greg B. Smith, "NYCHA nightmare: More Than 800
    Kids Tainted by Lead, de Blasio Administration Finally
    Concedes," New York Daily News, June 30, 2018

3   David Harvey, Rebel Cities: From The Right to The City to
    the Urban Revolution (Verso, London, 2012), 7-8

4   D. Bradford Hunt, Blueprint for Disaster: The Unraveling
    of Chicago Public Housing (University of Chicago Press,
    Chicago, 2009), 20-1

5   Nicholas Dagen Bloom, Public Housing that Worked: New
    York in the Twentieth Century (University of Pennsylvania
    Press. Philadelphia, 2008), 88

6   Owen Hatherley, Militant Modernism (Zero Books,
    Hampshire, 2009), Kindle Edition, Loc. 99

7   Nathan Glazer, From a Cause to a Style: Modernist

Architecture's Encounter with the American City (Princeton University Press, New Jersey, 2007), 7

8   Edwin G. Goetz, New Deal Ruins: Race, Economic Justice, and Public Housing Policy (Cornell University Press, New York, 2013), Kindle Edition Loc

9   Robert Venturi, Complexity and Contradiction in Architecture (The Museum of Modern Art, 1966), 16

10   Tom Wolfe, From Bauhaus to Our House (Bantam, New York, 1981), 53

11   Charles Jenaks, The Language of Post-Modern Architecture (4th ed) (Rizzoni, 1988), 9

12   Goetz, New Deal Ruins, Kindle Edition Loc. 862

13   Fritz Umbach and Alexander Gerould, Myth#3: Public Housing Breeds Crime in Public Housing Myths: Perception, Reality, and Social Policy (Cornell University Press, New York, 2015), 84

14   Bradford Hunt, Myth#2: Modernist Architecture Failed Public Housing, in Public Housing Myths: Perception, Reality, and Social Policy (Cornell University Press, New York, 2015), 56-7

15   Hunt, Blueprint for Disaster, 151

16   Ben Austen, High-Rises: Cabrini-Green and the Fate of American Public Housing (Harper, New York, 2018), Kindle Edition Loc. 4937

17   Ben Austen, High-Rises, Kindle Edition Loc. 4452

18   Gerald P. Marquis and Soumen Ghosh, Housing Opportunities for People Everywhere (HOPE VI): Who gets back in?, The Social Science Journal 45(3): 401-18, September 2008

19   Goetz, New Deal Ruins, Kindle Edition Loc. 3145; Stephanie Garlock, "By 2011, Atlanta Had Demolished All of Its Public Housing Projects. Where Did All Those People Go," Citylab, May 8, 2014

20   The Urban Institute and Brookings Institute, A Decade of

HOPE VI, 40, available online https://www.urban.org/sites/default/files/alfresco/publication-pdfs/411002-A-Decade-of-HOPE-VI.PDF

21 Hunt, Blueprint for Disaster, 254

22 Lance Freeman, There Goes the 'Hood: Views of Gentrification From The Ground Up (Temple University Press, Philadelphia, 2006), 133

23 Gale Holland, "LA's homelessness surged 75% in six years. Here's why the crisis has been decades in the making," LA Times, Feb 1st, 2018

24 Ryan Cooper and Peter Cowen, "Social Housing is the Answer," Jacobin, April 5, 2018

25 Lawrence J. Vale, Myth#6: Mixed-Income Redevelopment is the Only Way to Fix Failed Public Housing in Public Housing Myths, 149

26 Glazer, From a Cause to a Style, 285

CULTURE, SOCIETY & POLITICS

The modern world is at an impasse. Disasters scroll across our smartphone screens and we're invited to like, follow or upvote, but critical thinking is harder and harder to find. Rather than connecting us in common struggle and debate, the internet has sped up and deepened a long-standing process of alienation and atomization. Zer0 Books wants to work against this trend. With critical theory as our jumping off point, we aim to publish books that make our readers uncomfortable. We want to move beyond received opinions.

Zer0 Books is on the left and wants to reinvent the left. We are sick of the injustice, the suffering, and the stupidity that defines both our political and cultural world, and we aim to find a new foundation for a new struggle.

If this book has helped you to clarify an idea, solve a problem or extend your knowledge, you may want to check out our online content as well. Look for Zer0 Books: Advancing Conversations in the iTunes directory and for our Zer0 Books YouTube channel.

Popular videos include:
Žižek and the Double Blackmain
The Intellectual Dark Web is a Bad Sign
Can there be an Anti-SJW Left?
Answering Jordan Peterson on Marxism
Follow us on Facebook
at https://www.facebook.com/ZeroBooks and Twitter at https://twitter.com/Zer0Books

Bestsellers from Zer0 Books include:

Give Them An Argument
Logic for the Left
Ben Burgis
Many serious leftists have learned to distrust talk of logic. This is
a serious mistake.
Paperback: 978-1-78904-210-8 ebook: 978-1-78904-211-5

Poor but Sexy
Culture Clashes in Europe East and West
Agata Pyzik
How the East stayed East and the West stayed West.
Paperback: 978-1-78099-394-2 ebook: 978-1-78099-395-9

An Anthropology of Nothing in Particular
Martin Demant Frederiksen
A journey into the social lives of meaninglessness.
Paperback: 978-1-78535-699-5 ebook: 978-1-78535-700-8

In the Dust of This Planet
Horror of Philosophy vol. 1
Eugene Thacker
In the first of a series of three books on the Horror of Philosophy,
In the Dust of This Planet offers the genre of horror as a way of
thinking about the unthinkable.
Paperback: 978-1-84694-676-9 ebook: 978-1-78099-010-1

The End of Oulipo?
An Attempt to Exhaust a Movement
Lauren Elkin, Veronica Esposito
Paperback: 978-1-78099-655-4 ebook: 978-1-78099-656-1

Capitalist Realism
Is There no Alternative?
Mark Fisher
An analysis of the ways in which capitalism has presented itself
as the only realistic political-economic system.
Paperback: 978-1-84694-317-1 ebook: 978-1-78099-734-6

Rebel Rebel
Chris O'Leary
David Bowie: every single song. Everything you want to know,
everything you didn't know.
Paperback: 978-1-78099-244-0 ebook: 978-1-78099-713-1

Kill All Normies
Angela Nagle
Online culture wars from 4chan and Tumblr to Trump.
Paperback: 978-1- 78535-543-1 ebook: 978-1-78535-544-8

Cartographies of the Absolute
Alberto Toscano, Jeff Kinkle
An aesthetics of the economy for the twenty-first century.
Paperback: 978-1-78099-275-4 ebook: 978-1-78279-973-3

Malign Velocities
Accelerationism and Capitalism
Benjamin Noys
Long listed for the Bread and Roses Prize 2015, *Malign Velocities*
argues against the need for speed, tracking acceleration
as the symptom of the ongoing crises of capitalism.
Paperback: 978-1-78279-300-7 ebook: 978-1-78279-299-4

Meat Market
Female Flesh under Capitalism
Laurie Penny
A feminist dissection of women's bodies as the fleshy fulcrum of
capitalist cannibalism, whereby women are both consumers and
consumed.
Paperback: 978-1-84694-521-2 ebook: 978-1-84694-782-7

Babbling Corpse
Vaporwave and the Commodification of Ghosts
Grafton Tanner
Paperback: 978-1-78279-759-3 ebook: 978-1-78279-760-9

New Work New Culture
Work we want and a culture that strengthens us
Frithjoff Bergmann
A serious alternative for mankind and the planet.
Paperback: 978-1-78904-064-7 ebook: 978-1-78904-065-4

Romeo and Juliet in Palestine
Teaching Under Occupation
Tom Sperlinger
Life in the West Bank, the nature of pedagogy and the role of a
university under occupation.
Paperback: 978-1-78279-637-4 ebook: 978-1-78279-636-7

Ghosts of My Life
Writings on Depression, Hauntology and Lost Futures
Mark Fisher
Paperback: 978-1-78099-226-6 ebook: 978-1-78279-624-4

Sweetening the Pill
or How We Got Hooked on Hormonal Birth Control
Holly Grigg-Spall
Has contraception liberated or oppressed women?
Sweetening the Pill breaks the silence on the dark side of hormonal contraception.
Paperback: 978-1-78099-607-3 ebook: 978-1-78099-608-0

Why Are We The Good Guys?
Reclaiming your Mind from the Delusions of Propaganda
David Cromwell
A provocative challenge to the standard ideology that Western power is a benevolent force in the world.
Paperback: 978-1-78099-365-2 ebook: 978-1-78099-366-9

The Writing on the Wall
On the Decomposition of Capitalism and its Critics
Anselm Jappe, Alastair Hemmens
A new approach to the meaning of social emancipation.
Paperback: 978-1-78535-581-3 ebook: 978-1-78535-582-0

Enjoying It
Candy Crush and Capitalism
Alfie Bown
A study of enjoyment and of the enjoyment of studying. Bown asks what enjoyment says about us and what we say about enjoyment, and why.
Paperback: 978-1-78535-155-6 ebook: 978-1-78535-156-3

Color, Facture, Art and Design
Iona Singh
This materialist definition of fine-art develops guidelines for architecture, design, cultural-studies and ultimately social change.
Paperback: 978-1-78099-629-5 ebook: 978-1-78099-630-1

Neglected or Misunderstood
The Radical Feminism of Shulamith Firestone
Victoria Margree
An interrogation of issues surrounding gender, biology,
sexuality, work and technology, and the ways in which our
imaginations continue to be in thrall to ideologies of maternity
and the nuclear family.
Paperback: 978-1-78535-539-4 ebook: 978-1-78535-540-0

How to Dismantle the NHS in 10 Easy Steps (Second Edition)
Youssef El-Gingihy
The story of how your NHS was sold off and why you will have
to buy private health insurance soon. A new expanded second
edition with chapters on junior doctors' strikes and government
blueprints for US-style healthcare.
Paperback: 978-1-78904-178-1 ebook: 978-1-78904-179-8

Digesting Recipes
The Art of Culinary Notation
Susannah Worth
A recipe is an instruction, the imperative tone of the expert, but
this constraint can offer its own kind of potential. A recipe need
not be a domestic trap but might instead offer escape – something
to fantasise about or aspire to.
Paperback: 978-1-78279-860-6 ebook: 978-1-78279-859-0

Most titles are published in paperback and as an ebook.
Paperbacks are available in traditional bookshops. Both print and
ebook formats are available online.
Follow us on Facebook
at https://www.facebook.com/ZeroBooks
and Twitter at https://twitter.com/Zer0Books